WHAT'S NEXT?

NAVIGATING LIFE AFTER COLLEGE

CHRIS ZEIGLER

For my wife, who always challenges me to dream bigger than I could on my own, and my parents who have always believed in me and taught me what it means to live as a Christ follower.

CONTENTS

INTRODUCTION

Congrats! You made it. After four long years (or five, or six, but really who's counting?), sleepless all-nighters to write papers you put off until the very last minute and much more pizza than a nutrition major would ever recommend, you graduated college.

So, by now you've got a good job lined up with decent benefits, a budget mapped out, and you're ready to start climbing the corporate ladder to success. Right?

Before you lose your lunch over that last paragraph – relax. I've got good news for you. If you don't have a life plan and you're not really sure what comes next, then you're actually doing it right. Sure, it's great to have dreams and goals and be someone who takes action, but most of us spend our twenties just trying to figure out who we are and what we want out of life. You might have thought you'd have all that figured out after college, but most of us need more than just four years to get to that point.

As I write this, I am married with three children and working as the Director for a college ministry in the

Northeast. We live in a two thousand person town with one stop light and two gas stations. My wife and I joke that it's probably the only town in the United States smaller than the one we grew up in.

The point is, when I graduated college I didn't plan for any of those things to happen. The only one I was expecting was to marry my high school sweetheart. I could never have predicted or planned that God was going to lead me to where I am now.

From the time we're young, we feel pressure from our parents and others to figure it all out by the time we go to college so that we can graduate and make something of ourselves. It sounds realistic that we should be able to have some sort of plan in place by the time we've experienced eighteen years of life, but when you're unable to find a job in your field and you're stuck working in retail, you get discouraged. Even worse, maybe you have found a job in your field and after feeling unsatisfied and unhappy you are left wondering why you made the decisions that you did. The questions begin to pile up like that mountain of student loans you feel like you'll be paying off for the rest of your life.

We have been told there's a formula that if followed correctly will lead to success in life. You must work hard and be a good student so you can get into college. Then work hard again to get good grades in college, get an internship or two, maybe be an RA at school, and do other extracurricular activities so you'll have plenty to make your résumé stand out. Once you submit that resumé to every possible place you can think of, you'll land a great job, eventually meet the love of your life, settle down with your two children and a dog, and just like that you will have found success!

But when you look at some of the most successful people, you'll often hear a different story. Most of their stories don't follow a linear progression at all. And many of them don't define success as being married with two kids and a dog while working a monotonous job saving for retirement.

Successful people don't play life like a chess game, stressing over making perfectly timed moves, but more like jazz musicians, seeing where the music goes and then improvising in the moment. I've found that life is a lot less like a precise math equation and much more like an evolving piece of music. It's more about self-discovery and less about making the perfectly timed move.

Before I get too ahead of myself, let me add a disclaimer. It may sound like I'm going to advocate for just letting life happen to you, but that is not true at all. I firmly believe in setting goals, laying out plans, and taking action to see great things happen in your life. In fact, we'll talk about that at one point later in this book.

But often we think that if life were mapped out for us and we could just follow the map from point A to point B, then that would be the best solution. That is not how life works. Life's beauty comes from the unexpected. It comes from experiencing ups and downs and it comes from figuring things out as we go.

INTRODUCTION

Did you ever read those *Choose Your Own Adventure* books as a child? I remember reading those books and getting to a place where I could decide what direction to take next in the story. Now, for the over-analytical readers, these choices were probably daunting as they carefully thought through the ramifications of each decision (or maybe they just looked ahead and cheated), but for me there was an excitement in getting to decide what direction I wanted the story to go. I loved that there was no wrong or right answer in that moment. It was simply a chance to discover something new. And life can be a lot like that as well.

The problem is for many who graduate college, they don't know where to begin. They still have some work to do in finding themselves and discovering where they want to go. So, as we discuss how to navigate your twenties, we'll start with small goals that lead you to self-discovery and a better understanding of who you are and what you want out of life. To start I'll talk a lot about the types of feelings and thoughts you will encounter, and then I'll give you some practical steps from what I've learned for how to navigate these years and come out better equipped to live out your personal purpose. Along with my story, we'll look at what we can learn from the lives of the biblical characters Moses and Joshua. You might be surprised to find out that much of what they went through can apply to what we experience in our twenties.

So, if you're ready to learn more, let's dig in!

YOU WON'T ALWAYS
BE A WANDERER

M ike and Kelly sat across the table from my wife, me, and our two young children, who were turning our peaceful dinner into what I imagine feeding time at the zoo looks and sounds like. We talked over homemade macaroni and cheese and chicken nuggets, a meal that I can get away with eating as a grown adult now that I have kids. Mike and Kelly had been married a couple of months out of college and moved into an apartment down the hall. As I spoke with them, they buzzed with excitement like high schoolers during their first week of summer vacation.

Being the exemplary neighbors that my wife and I are, we had invited Mike and Kelly over to enjoy a meal and to get to know them better. The topic of conversation bounced around from how good my wife's cooking is, to our different family backgrounds, to how they were enjoying married life. After getting into what seemed like a hostage negotiation with our picky daughter over her dinner (what kid doesn't like macaroni and cheese and

1

chicken nuggets?), we landed on the subject of jobs and the directions life will take you.

Mike had recently been promoted from host to a server position at a nearby restaurant and Kelly was working as a fill-in secretary. She had been hired to fill the position of another woman who would be moving on, but with that change still about a year off, she was feeling a little out of place. We transitioned to the living room, where, now that the war over dinner had passed, my children suddenly went back to being well-behaved and enjoyable. As we sat on separate couches discussing life after college, I was reminded of the uncertainty that followed such an amazing experience.

I remember life just after graduation. Following an internship, I was blessed to get a job in my field working at a local television station. I went to school to work in television production, so getting to jump right into working on a news set was encouraging. It would have been the perfect first gig if not for the 5 a.m. start time and the 45-minute commute due to where I was living at the time.

But, it was a job in my field and most people don't get that right out of college. I've seen many post-grads struggle with transitioning to an 8 or 9 a.m. work schedule after having years of staying up till all hours of the morning, but 5 a.m. was a whole different ballgame. As someone who refused to drink soda or energy drinks in the morning and who hates the taste of coffee, I would pull myself out of bed and try to find some way to motivate myself for the long drive. If it's true that we all have guardian angels, then mine must have been busier that summer than a medic at the X Games.

I would stumble into work trying to force my eyes open and then sit down with people who had been doing this for years – some of them for decades. I understood that sacrifices needed to be made when you're first out of college, but I quickly learned that waking up before roosters wasn't one I was willing to make for long. It also didn't help that over those few months I realized working in broadcast news was boring and repetitive. With my wedding only a couple of months off, I began scrambling to find other full-time work and subsequently prayed around the clock.

It wasn't that I completely hated my job, but more that I valued my life. I had been raised by parents who taught me the value of working hard, so it wasn't that I was being lazy or trying to escape hard work. No, it had more to do with the fact that I could tell this wasn't the direction I was supposed to take in life. I could tell that I wasn't going to find fulfillment at this job. Sure, I could continue to stick it out, and if I really believed God had told me to, I would have. But I knew it wasn't something worth spending time on unless this was where God wanted me to be. And again, I was desperately aware that I needed to find something more steady as I was heading towards marriage.

Right up there with car shopping, job hunting and going on interviews may be two of the least enjoyable parts of adulthood. I really have no reason to complain, though, because after just a couple of months I was able to find my next job working at a small public television station in central New York state. Thankfully, I had done an internship there as well and that had opened doors for me. While it paid a meager salary, sponsored in part by viewers like you, I was optimistic and it seemed like the formula was paying off.

I had gone to school, worked hard, and earned a good degree. Now here I was, after a couple of short internships in my senior year, with a full-time job in my field right out of college, and I was just about to marry the love of my life.

Rewind back to my living room with Mike and Kelly and here they were discussing how to make some of those same hard decisions that I had to make at that time in life. They were expressing how concerned they were about making big decisions in this season and how that would influence the rest of their lives. I listened as Kelly shared concerns about trying to make the right decisions so that everything would turn out the best in the end. In short, they wanted to know they had it all figured out.

It's a desire we all have really. No one likes the idea of uncertainty when it comes to planning out your life. Remember when you had to choose a college major or determine what school you would go to? Sometimes we feel like we've got a good handle on everything, but more often we find ourselves questioning every move we make and worrying about the outcome. That's exactly where Mike and Kelly found themselves that night in our living room.

There is a secret I shared with them in that conversation that I want to share with you, too. If you're not sure exactly what your life is supposed to look like, then you're actually doing it right. If you feel like you're still trying to figure it out, that's okay. Maybe that statement is reassuring for you or maybe you're wondering why you shelled out some cash just to get such a vague piece of advice. For Mike and Kelly, it was relieving when I shared that "secret." Their shoulders relaxed and the tension was gone. It was as if a peace treaty was signed to bring an end to the barrage of thoughts they had been battling for months.

I'm not someone who's much of a chess player, but when I have played in the past, I would become irritated as I carefully deliberated over every move. There was no fun in the game for me, which is probably why I'm not much of a chess player now. But when I learned more about the intricacies of the game, it completely changed my perspective. Because each player starts with 16 pieces and each piece has its own rules concerning what moves it can make, the possibilities are practically endless. This is what can be both terrifying about the game and freeing at the same time.

As the game of chess goes on, the number of potential moves actually increases. After each player has taken one turn, there are 400 possible ways the game could go. After the second pair of moves, there are 197,742 ways the game could go. And by the completion of the third turn, 121 million possibilities exist. In fact, there are more possible games of chess than there are atoms in the universe.[1] The first move can seem intimidating because there are so many possibilities, but, on the other hand, there are so many possibilities that if you make a mistake, there are nearly an infinite number of ways to fix it. Life is very similar to chess. With an infinite number of possibilities, we can get so caught up worrying about the first move that we become paralyzed with fear and neglect to make a move at all.

Sometimes all we need is to be reassured that we're not going to screw up our lives with one bad decision (unless it's the kind that lands you in jail), but rather that we can move forward one step at a time, trusting that God has our best in mind. No decision you make will ever catch God off guard. In fact, David writes in the Psalms about God, "all the days ordained for me were written in your book before one of them came to be" (Psalm 139:16, NIV). One of the great paradoxes of life is that we have the freedom to make our own choices and, yet, God knows which ones we will make before we choose.

I have discovered over the years that when I relax, trust God, and seek Him, the pressure I have felt subsides. You see, if God has already ordained all my days, then there's no pressure for *me* to get everything just right. No, in actuality, the pressure is on God to lead me in the right direction and to provide for me along the way. Something tells me that He handles the pressure far better than I ever would.

Here's another helpful thing to note. If you find yourself at a crossroads and aren't sure what path to take, then you can identify with pretty much every person God has used in amazing ways throughout history. Take Moses for example. Here's a guy whose life direction was uncertain right from the beginning. He was a Hebrew boy born in Egypt at a time when Pharaoh (the king) had declared that all Hebrew boys should be put to death out of fear that their rapid population growth would eventually overtake the Egyptians.

Aware of this decree, his mother chose to place him in a basket and let the basket float down the Nile River. I've always found this part of the story quite strange. I imagine that Moses' mother either had great faith in God or was a little crazy. Either way, if this were to happen today, you can bet CPS would be all over it. But God had a plan in all of this. Moses was found by the princess, Pharaoh's daughter, who chose to raise him in the palace. There's irony for you – a boy who was supposed to be killed out of fear that the Hebrews might overrun the kingdom was now being brought up in the king's palace.

As Moses grew up in the palace with every luxury available to him, his people were forced to work hard as slaves to the Egyptian kingdom. One day while walking among the people, he came upon an Egyptian beating one of the Hebrews. And this is where Moses' life takes an unexpected turn. This is where things go a direction that he never anticipated. Overcome with anger at the sight of this, Moses took matters into his own hands. After looking around to make sure no one was watching, he killed the Egyptian man and buried his body in the sand.

The next day Moses decided to go out among the people again and when he saw two Hebrew slaves fighting he tried to break it up. But when Moses intervened one of the men said to him, "'Who made you a prince and a judge over us? Do you mean to kill me as you killed the Egyptian?'" (Exodus 2:14, ESV). With this Moses realized people were aware of his secret, so he fled to the desert in fear.

In just a day's time Moses had gone from living the high life in the palace of the greatest empire on earth to wandering alone in the desert fearing for his life. I've tried to imagine how Moses must have felt when that happened. After all, the reason he was homeless was because he did what he thought was the right thing by coming to the defense of someone being wrongfully assaulted.

I'm sure there were a million thoughts going through his mind as he replayed what had happened. He must have thought: Why didn't I just let that man fight his own battle? Why am I out here in the desert when I did the right thing? Doesn't God see me? And while Moses now found himself in a pretty bad situation, he had unknowingly stumbled upon his purpose.

I believe that when Moses saw that Egyptian beating the Hebrew man, a simultaneous burst of anger and compassion rose up in him because God had placed a desire deep in Moses' heart to rescue His people. The problem was, Moses wasn't ready for that kind of responsibility yet and the way that he chose to respond, by committing murder, wasn't God's way. Moses had discovered his purpose, but he hadn't yet submitted his heart to God. And now he found himself wandering in the wilderness.

Maybe you can relate to Moses – hopefully not in the I-killed-a-man-beating-a-slave kind of way, but more in the sense that you're looking for your purpose, or may have even found it, and still feel like you're wandering in the desert. I'm in my 30's, and while I definitely have a better understanding of where God's taking me, I must confess that I still feel like a wanderer at times. In my twenties, I held five different career positions at three different companies, became a husband and then a father, and changed my mind about what I thought my purpose was more times than I can count.

Life can take unexpected turns and before you know it, you feel like you're wandering – like you're trying to navigate life alone and you can't even see down the road past all the fog. Maybe you have felt that way before when that guy or girl you thought you would marry suddenly broke up with you. Or maybe a loved one passed away unexpectedly. Or maybe you decided to change majors in college and faced the fear and uncertainty that goes along with that.

In 2009, my life took an unexpected turn that brought a lot of uncertainty with it. I had been grinding away working at that little public television station. It sure beat waking up before 5 a.m., but it hadn't brought the fulfillment I had expected either. An opportunity arose when I was asked to be the first assistant director for a big project they were doing. The plan was to create a show for kids that would be fun like a sitcom and teach science at the same time. The company was going to create a pilot episode and then pitch the show to major networks in the hopes that one of them would pick it up for a full series.

As I worked on the project, I became close friends with the producer and director, and we began to dream of what the show could become. We talked about filming the volcanoes in Hawaii and the Great Barrier Reef in Australia. We dreamed about the six-figure incomes we could make and how we would spend that money. After a 90-hour work week for filming and months of editing later, they started pitching it to other film studios.

Time went by, and although there was a lot of promise, the company I worked for didn't handle parts of the process well. It looked like things weren't going to pan out. At the same time, I was praying regularly because I knew that the best place for me to be was where God wanted me, whether that was working on the show or doing something different. My prayer became, "God, I'll go wherever you tell me to go and do whatever you tell me to do." Deep down I wanted to do God's will more than anything else and looking back, this became the most important prayer I would ever pray.

Through a series of events that included attending our old college ministry group and then going to a conference for young adults, my wife and I felt that God was leading us into full-time ministry working with college students. Neither one of us had ever expected to find ourselves in ministry, but here we were. This position we were planning to take required us to raise our own salary by asking friends and family to support us monthly like missionaries, and we would need to move out of our hometown where we had lived our whole lives. It was quite the unexpected change.

So, we left behind our friends and family, we left behind the idea of a six-figure income, and we left behind pretty much everything we had known. Uncertainty has a way of bringing out fear in people, which I'm sure Moses experienced, but we were grateful that even as we moved into a new season we had an assurance that this was what God called us to. There's something very calming about hearing God's voice, even when you don't know exactly what the end result will look like. We hadn't heard Him audibly, but He had confirmed through our prayers and others' that this was right and we had a deep sense of peace in the choice we were making.

I bet that being in the desert was no fun for Moses. All his time living in the palace probably didn't prepare him well for scavenging and trying to fight off the kinds of beasts he would encounter. And if you're in "a wilderness" right now, then you probably don't feel like your parents or schooling prepared you adequately for this moment either. Maybe, like me, you graduated college with certain expectations. Many of us are told that if we follow a formula, it will lead to happiness and success. If we can work hard enough, get good grades, and do well in college, then our lives will be full of satisfaction.

The problem with that mindset is that life is not a paint-by-number. Do you remember those activities as a child? There was a picture broken up into different pieces and each piece had a number in it. If you followed the key filling in each section with the color it said, your picture would turn out looking great. They were perfect for someone like me who had no clue what I was doing when it came to art class.

But I did the formulaic paint-by-number lifestyle and found myself unsatisfied. I graduated with a degree and a pretty good GPA. I married the woman of my dreams and even landed a job in my field right out of college. But all those things couldn't bring the satisfaction that comes from living a life surrendered to God. And it was when I surrendered my plans to Him and prayed that prayer, "I'll go wherever you want me to go and do whatever you want me to do," that God graciously pointed me in a completely different direction than the one I had for my life. And when He did that, I began to feel more fulfilled than ever.

You see, I've known many young people who agonize over finding God's will for their lives. They have such a great desire to walk with God and do what He wants, but they chase after the perfect answer like it's this mystical genie in a bottle that they'll never come across. God's will for your life isn't this far-off mystery that will only be made known through an oracle. This isn't the *Lord of the Rings*. This is your life and the answers are quite simple to find really, if you surrender your heart and actions completely to Him and are willing to pray that same risky prayer that I did.

That doesn't mean you'll immediately know everything that you're going to do with your life. When my wife and I made the decision to go into full-time college ministry, it didn't really make sense to us. But just because we couldn't make sense of it with *our* limited understanding, doesn't mean it didn't make sense. God knows what He is doing and I believe that God purposely reveals things to us in pieces because He knows that dependency on Him helps us grow. And God will take those pieces of your life and create a masterpiece, if you'll let Him. That masterpiece will look far more beautiful than any paint-by-number could.

Have you ever watched a skilled artist work? You'd think they would be very neat and methodical, but often their work is confusing and paint goes everywhere. To the outside observer it would look like they have no idea what they're doing, but the artist has something in mind that he is already working to create. He sees the whole picture, but we don't.

Maybe you've been saying, "God, I don't know what to do. I don't know where to go or what you have planned for me and I need to hear from you!" When you surrender yourself to Him completely, maybe by praying that prayer of surrender that I did, He will begin to direct you by opening and closing doors in your life much like he did with leading my wife and me into ministry to college students. While it may feel like an agonizing journey to get there, as I look back on my twenties, there's something important I've realized.

I won't always be a wanderer.

God doesn't do anything by mistake and you are no exception. The Bible tells us that He knows the plans He has for us before we are even born. You may feel like a wanderer now, but let me assure you that is not the case. Nothing you do goes unseen by your heavenly Father. Nothing that happens is beyond His control. It's okay if there are times when you feel like you always will be a wanderer – like you'll never figure life out and things will never line up for you. But God has given you an exhilarating, wonderful, and possibly life-altering purpose.

You may not know what it is yet. It may even take you a decade or more to figure it out, but God has put something deep within each of us that He wants to use to shape the world. That's the difference between a paint by number and something like Vincent van Gogh's *Starry Night*. The steps along the way will most likely be messy and may feel unordered or confusing, but it's worth it for the wonderful masterpiece that God wants to create with your life. One feels safe, reliable and ... boring. The other feels much riskier, possibly even dangerous, but is more like the life that Jesus lived.

The key is trusting that God is in the process and has been all along.

GOOD FRUIT TAKES TIME

Have you ever been called impatient? As a child, I was dubbed the impatient one in the family. I tried to tell my parents that the problem with being patient is all the darn waiting it requires. My impatience soon became a running joke in our family. Whenever we would have to wait in line at the grocery store or when dinner wasn't ready at the normal time, I'd express my frustration that was met with a chorus of "Stop being so impatient!" from my family members.

I've gotten much better in my adult years. There's nothing like having patience forced upon you by a toddler who can't use words to communicate what he or she wants. And so my patience has grown over time, but a couple of years back I embarked upon (was tricked into, really) an endeavor that would test my patience significantly.

We were told that residents in the apartment complex we lived in could grow a garden during the summer months. I've never been one for gardening. The idea of pulling weeds under the hot sun for hours makes me sick. But being the loving (and foolish) husband I am, when my wife begged me to plant some seeds with her for fresh produce, I acquiesced. She convinced me that the garden would be small and would not require much work. She lied. Every day we had to go out and water the ground, often twice a day, and then we needed to pull weeds. I swear, if you ever want to know what the ninth circle of hell is like, picture a garden that needs weeding when it's 95 degrees outside while Satan peers over you with a pitchfork, but stands just enough out of the way to ensure there's no shade.

But the worst part about a garden is how long it takes to see results. I've always been a results driven person, and so as we labored day after day for what felt like an eternity, I was anxious to see progress. For each day that went by weeding, watering, bathing in sweat, and questioning why I loved my wife so much that I would let her do this to me, it seemed there was nothing to show for it. Weeks went by and still all we could see was a patch of dirt. Brown, boring, lifeless dirt.

Finally, after some time, shoots began to spring up. The work that had been happening underneath the soil began to break through and produce the visible results I had been longing for. The produce my wife had been so excited for and we had worked so hard to grow started to come forth. In a few more weeks, the garden was teeming with colors as tomatoes, zucchinis, pumpkins, lettuce, and yellow squash began to form.

I wish I could tell you that the end of this story is a happy one. I wish I could share with you that we ate gluttonous vegetable filled meals to our heart's content. But alas, the deer in our area were even more excited about our garden than we were, and despite our best efforts to keep them out, including my wife's attempt to hang a noose (her hatred for deer runs deep), they ate more of the produce from that garden than we did. Since then, she and I have come to an agreement that we will spend the budget we used on that garden at the local farmer's market and leave the sweating and weed pulling up to others.

The point is, we live in a *now* culture. We can do almost everything in the blink of an eye. In fact, we expect it, which is really great for people like me. I can pull up any movie or TV show on Netflix and start watching instantly. With Apple Pay you can pay for your food at a McDonald's or buy your groceries in less than five seconds. I feel so cool when I do that. And if a website doesn't load in two seconds or less, something is wrong with my Internet connection. But even with all these technological advances, some things never change. Whether it's growing your own garden or going to an apple orchard, if you want good fruit, it takes time.

Jesus talked about this principle, saying, "I am the true vine, and my Father is the gardener. He cuts off every branch in me that bears no fruit, while every branch that does bear fruit He prunes so that it will be even more fruitful" (John 15:1-2, NIV). What Jesus is communicating here is that pruning leads to blooming. We want fruit in our lives and we want to see it right away, but to bear fruit, Jesus says we must be pruned first. No one likes pruning, but it's not as terrible as you might think (even though it might not feel great at the time).

When Jesus talks about pruning, it's really a picture of the Father lifting up unproductive vines off of the ground (as is common in taking care of a vineyard), that they may get more sun and bear fruit better. If you're tending a grapevine, you actually have to train the vines to go the way you want them to. That's why vineyards look the way they do with the vines in neat rows and up off the ground. It's because the owner of the vineyard has used stakes and wire to train the vines. In the same way, God is patiently training us so that we will grow, be more productive, and bear better fruit. He knows that good fruit takes time – that pruning leads to blooming.

Joseph is the perfect Biblical example of this. God gave him big dreams and visions of the future, but his character wasn't quite established yet. In the book of Genesis, we read that when Joseph dreamed that his older siblings were bowing down to him, he used no discretion in telling them so. He displayed enthusiasm and eagerness to tell his brothers about this. I picture Joseph like that annoying little kid who always thinks he's the best at everything.

It would take many years and many pruning events: sold into slavery, thrown into prison, and appointed to major responsibilities in Egypt, to cut back his pride and to shape his character. Yet at the end of his life, Joseph bore the fruit of such pruning. He was a wise, humble, and kind leader. Eventually, he did rule over his older brothers, and in his father's dying blessing, he pronounced that, "Joseph was a fruitful vine" (Genesis 49:22, NIV).

While pruning can be difficult, as with Joseph, you can find refuge in knowing that God is working in your waiting. I'm thankful that God is so patient with me. He's definitely more patient with me than I was with my garden. He's more patient with me than I am with myself most of the time.

A little while back I learned about how giant bamboo grows. Giant bamboo requires a lot more patience than my small backyard garden. The first year you plant seeds, water, and tend to the bamboo, and when the growing season is over, you have nothing to show for it – not even a tiny green sprout. If you haven't given up, you come back the next year making sure to take care of the plant and cultivate it well to see three to six inches of growth.

Now, if I made it this far (and based on my previous gardening experience, I wouldn't), I'd be pretty discouraged at this point. But for those who are more patient than I am and press on, the bamboo reaches a height of six to twelve inches in its third year. And in its fourth year, it reaches twelve to eighteen inches. Can you imagine pouring hours of labor into something for four straight years with so little to show for your efforts? Just the thought of it makes me feel depressed, but for those who are willing to stick it out for another year something incredible happens.

In year five, the bamboo experiences massive growth to the point where it can develop up to three feet *per day*! Imagine coming out to check on your bamboo to find that in one day it has grown double the rate of what it grew in four years! And from that point on, the bamboo continues to grow rapidly until some can surpass 100 feet tall. This blows my mind. I'm convinced that if everyone on the planet was like me, we would never have discovered the value of giant bamboo because it would never have gotten to this point!

You see, over the course of those first four years, the bamboo is putting down roots and establishing itself so that it can sustain the incredible growth that takes place in the fifth year. Sometimes we get so concerned with what we need to do (the outward fruit) that we forget to focus on growing our character (the inward roots) first. All the while that we're looking for fruit, God is looking to develop our roots. And while we think very little is happening in our lives, if we will submit ourselves to Him, we'll see that God is working in us and doing something powerful to prepare us for what's next. My pastor put it this way, "We crave miracles and momentum, but God wants maturity."

I've learned over the years that God cares more about developing our character than He does about us doing the right things. He knows that good character in our lives leads to right actions. If you think about the other Biblical passage famous for talking about fruit, it's when Paul talks about how the fruits of the Spirit are love, joy, peace, patience, kindness, goodness, faithfulness, gentleness, and self-control. All of these are inward things that develop our character and then produce good fruit outwardly. This is exactly what God was getting at with Moses when he killed the Egyptian. Moses' intentions (to protect God's people) were right, but his character and the way he went about it were all wrong.

We must first see internal growth before we can expect positive external results. Author Ruth Haley Barton puts it this way, "We set young leaders up for a fall if we encourage them to envision what they can do before they consider the kind of person they should be."[1]

In talking about the vineyard, Jesus goes on to say, "Abide in Me, and I in you. As the branch cannot bear fruit of itself unless it abides in the vine, so neither can you unless you abide in Me. I am the vine, you are the branches; he who abides in Me and I in him, he bears much fruit, for apart from Me you can do nothing" (John 15:4-5, NASB). It's important that we catch that last part. Apart from Jesus we can do nothing. Have you ever noticed that when we try to accomplish things on our own, it doesn't usually go as well as we think it will? We can end up failing and sometimes we hurt ourselves or others.

Don't hear me wrong – the Bible talks about the value of working hard and the pitfalls of laziness, but sometimes in our working hard, we try to force things and make them happen in our own strength. The Gospel isn't about self-sufficiency. In fact, it's about as far from that as we can get.

When Moses killed the Egyptian, he wasn't following God's plan for redeeming the Israelites. He was trying to accomplish it on his own and we can see how that worked out. Jesus is pointing out that there's no striving when you're abiding. When you are focused on Jesus and abiding in Him, you don't need to contend for things in your own power.

WE MUST FIRST SEE INTERNAL GROWTH BEFORE WE CAN EXPECT POSITIVE EXTERNAL RESULTS.

None of us likes uncertainty and so we do anything possible in our own power to prevent it. There have been many times that I have been praying in times of uncertainty and asking God to show me what His plans are for my life. I figure if He would just show me, things would be so much better. But it's in those times that He has come and said, "Chris, I can't show you the whole picture because you can't handle it. The plans I have for you are way beyond what you could dream or imagine on your own and if I tell you what they are, you'll try to accomplish them in your own strength." I know He's right and I also know that in doing so I would probably make a mess of it all.

One of my favorite portions of Scripture is in 2 Corinthians 12, when Paul is talking about the thorn in his side. We don't really know what the thorn is, but Paul tells us that he pleaded with God three times to take it away. God's reply to Paul was, "My grace is sufficient for you, for my power is made perfect in weakness" (2 Corinthians 12:9, ESV). What is God saying here? He's saying that there's no striving when you're abiding in Him.

We think of weakness as a bad thing. Certainly I do. But when I realized that God's power is perfected when I allow myself to be weak before Him, it completely changed my perspective. I began to see weakness as a good thing. It's still not something I look forward to, but it does mean that when I find myself in a place of weakness, instead of feeling frightened, I'm encouraged. Instead of feeling captive to fear, I feel a sense of freedom. Because I've found that things work best when I allow God to be God over my life. It's incredibly freeing when you give Him the responsibility of making your future great instead of carrying the burden yourself.

This has been a regular theme in my life at times that I've felt like God isn't moving fast enough or that I could just accomplish much more if He would just let me. As an impatient person, there have been several times when people have prayed for me, and as they did, they said they have seen a picture of me as a horse longing to run free. But they (yes, I've needed to hear this from multiple people because I can be stubborn) have expressed that God is putting the reins on me and using the bit and bridle (pieces that fit around a horse's head and mouth) to steer and guide me in the direction that God wants me to go. Over the years as I've been striving, often because I want to accomplish great things for God, He has graciously come to me and encouraged me to trust Him by whispering, "Let things come to you."

That's exactly what happened with Moses. He wasn't even thinking about rescuing the people of Israel from Pharaoh's oppressive rule when God came to him in the burning bush. By now he was married and had resolved himself to a simple life of tending sheep in the desert. But God had been working on his character and, unbeknownst to Moses, preparing him for what was next.

He had been learning how to survive in the desert, something that would come in handy when he led the Israelites into the wilderness. His work tending sheep would have developed the skills of patience and leadership he would need to guide God's flock. Who ever would have thought that God could teach Moses far more in the desert than he could in the palace? Who ever would have imagined that God would give him more influence as a shepherd than as a prince? Certainly not Moses.

In fact, when God came to Moses in the burning bush, he resisted the idea of going back to Egypt. His life had been turned upside down once already, and now that he had gotten used to being a shepherd, the idea of totally upending everything again was not exciting to him. You think you've got it bad because you can't figure out what direction to go in life? Here's Moses at the age of 80 and God wants to give him a whole new career that involves the dangers of challenging a king and trying to free the people who were the very reason his life had been overturned before!

You can't blame him for resisting another change that would bring loads of uncertainty, but what Moses couldn't see was that everything that had happened in his life was setting him up for this moment. Every plot twist in his storyline had been leading up to this paramount encounter with God in the burning bush. And whether you realize it or not, just as in the case of Moses, God is always at work in your life.

Recently, I woke up early to a beautiful summer morning. As I occasionally like to do, I decided to go for a walk and spend some time in prayer. I live in a tiny rural town about a 30-minute drive from the largest city in our area. In our one stoplight town, it's pretty quiet before 7 a.m. As I was walking, praying and enjoying the peace (something you value much more once you have children), I noticed a sound I hadn't heard before.

It was distant and faint, so much so that if there had even been the sound of a cricket I'm not sure I would have heard it. But as I strained my ears to hear what the sound could be, I realized that it was the noise of people on their morning commute to work in the city. As I listened more, I could make out the sound of beeping construction trucks and rumbling cars. In that moment I heard God say something profound that encouraged me, "Chris, whether you realize it or not, even when you can't hear it, even if it seems very far off, I am at work in your life."

So, how do we discern what God is up to in our lives even when it's hard to see Him at work? By abiding in Him. Let me quickly explain what I mean by that. Abiding in God, as Jesus commanded us in the book of John, means to stay connected to Him. This is the picture that Jesus gives us when He says that He is the vine and we are the branches. If a branch is disconnected from the vine, then it eventually dies and can't bear any fruit. We are called to stay connected to the Father and we can do that through reading the Bible and meditating on it, spending time in prayer talking with Him, trusting the Lord when difficult circumstances arise and loving others the way Christ modeled love for us. It's about seeing God as a friend we can form a relationship with instead of just an omnipotent, all-powerful, disconnected being.

The best way I have learned to determine what God is doing is through time spent in prayer talking with Him and then waiting and listening for His response. It's in those times I've heard God speak in ways that completely changed the course of my life. But waiting on God isn't always easy. Just ask the twelve disciples after Jesus went back to heaven.

The disciples had been hanging out with Jesus for over three years, and now that He had commissioned them to go out, I'm sure they were chomping at the bit to share the good news of the Gospel with every person possible. After being with Jesus every day, in person, for over three years, they probably felt ready to do the work they were called to do. I mean, they had just seen the greatest miracle in Jesus' crucifixion and resurrection!

But before Jesus left, He told the disciples to wait for the gift the Father had promised them. They didn't know when this gift would come, and they didn't even know what it would look like. Thankfully, by this time they had learned the value of obeying Jesus, because what would happen next was crucial to the ministry of the first church. The disciples had gone through years of pruning that led to this moment of blooming. All they had to do was cease striving and focus on abiding until the gift came.

As Jesus' closest followers gathered in an upstairs room, a powerful wind came from heaven and filled the whole house. Then what looked like tongues of fire rested above their heads, and they began to speak in other languages. This must have been a bizarre sight, but this was the Holy Spirit, the Helper, who had come just as Jesus had promised. And in that moment, they began to preach to everyone who would listen.

People from many different regions who spoke many different languages were there and each could understand what was being said in their own language. The Bible tells us that when Peter had finished speaking, over three thousand people chose to follow Christ that day! This was a defining moment because those new believers would help form the first church and aid in spreading the Gospel around the planet.

Now, can you imagine if the disciples had been impatient? Can you imagine if they had disregarded what Jesus said and tried to go out in their own strength? They most likely would have shared the Gospel with some, but three thousand people could have missed out on receiving the gift of salvation.

It's a good thing they had learned to wait patiently and trust that God knew better than they did. And just think, if it took the disciples over three years of being with Jesus every day to be prepared for their mission, how much longer might it take us for pruning to take place and good fruit to come forth?

When we want to run free and go after things on our own, when we believe that we can do things better when we do them our way, when impatience wants to force us into hasty decisions, we must remember that good fruit takes time. We must hold to the truth that God is working in our lives even when we don't see or understand it.

However, there are times when God will call us to make a move and go a different direction – just like he did with my wife and me when he called us into ministry with college students. He will use unexpected changes to continue developing your character as well. The important thing is to make moves for the right reasons.

So, before you rush to spend thousands of dollars on grad school or make a quick decision about a career move, stop and ask yourself this question, "Am I doing this out of impatience or because God has called me to it?" Whatever the answer to that question is, just remember: God loves you and wants what is best for you. Trusting His process can be difficult, but it will help you become your best in preparation for what lies ahead.

The principle of good fruit taking time doesn't mean you don't do anything or that your hands are tied for the rest of your life. Don't take it as your cue to avoid getting a job and live in your parents' basement the rest of your life. And if you're someone who is a go-getter, don't take it to mean that you'll never accomplish anything great either. It simply means that you surrender yourself to God's leading and trust Him to show you what's best instead of trying to make things happen in your own will and strength. The doing will come in time. When you have faithfully and patiently waited on Him, you'll most likely find yourself overwhelmed at all you have to do. But if you're still searching for that clear direction for your life, then the best thing you can do right now is to bloom where you're planted.

BLOOM WHERE
YOU'RE PLANTED

I n the case of Moses it took several decades and a lot
of pruning to develop his character and to reveal what
God had in mind for him. It was an encounter with
a burning bush that would finally call him out of the
wilderness. But that's the only thing everyone talks about.
What about the 40 years in between leaving Egypt and
seeing the burning bush? It's easy not to focus on his time
in the wilderness.

People don't usually share their stories of time in the
wilderness either. That's because we don't like to highlight
our failures or our seasons of meandering. We like to
put our best foot forward and talk about all the amazing
things we've accomplished once we've already come
through the wilderness. But it's important to pay attention
to the wilderness. Often it is in the wilderness that God
is most at work.

God used a wilderness experience in my life a couple
of years back to produce significant growth. I had been
working with college students for several years and

eventually was promoted to assistant director of the organization. It was a true honor and I was excited to take on this new role. After several years of holding that position, I learned that the executive director was planning to move on and that I could interview for his position.

As things unfolded over the course of a few weeks, I found out that another person in our organization who held a lower position than I did and had been at the company less time than I had would be interviewing as well. Even though I thought I was the best person for the job, I was a little nervous going into the interview with the board of directors. I felt like I had something to prove and wanted to show them that I was their best candidate.

There were late night conversations with my wife as the process continued, and I dreamed about all the things I would do if I were chosen as the next executive director. As I prayed, I believed God was behind me and that this was what I was supposed to do. I began to feel confident that I would get the position and excited about the direction I could take the ministry. But, as time went on, it began to look like I wouldn't get the job, and in the end my coworker was promoted over me and given the position. The board of directors was kind in letting me down by sharing that they wanted me to stay and that I was a good candidate for the job, just not the person they believed God wanted to lead the ministry at this time.

As you can imagine, that was an incredibly difficult time in my life. Here I was – I had been faithful in serving this organization for years, had been given a promotion to assistant director, and then in just a few months time was surpassed by someone who had less experience and, in my mind, fewer qualifications than I did. On top of that, this person was my friend, so it made the situation that much more awkward.

I decided I had two choices. I could accept my "defeat" and move on to a different organization. This is what I assume most people would have chosen. Or, I could stay where I was, swallow my pride, and continue to faithfully serve this organization and my new boss. That would certainly be the more challenging path, but something inside told me it was the right one. Every time I went to the Lord in prayer, He pointed me in this direction, too. I even heard Him tell me that this friend and I would be a one-two punch as leaders of our organization. That's a term used in boxing that means a punch with one hand followed by a punch from the side cross with the other hand. It's considered an especially effective combination.

So, after much deliberating, I made the choice to stay in my role as the assistant director. I'd like to say that it was an easy decision and that everything just clicked in my life from that moment on, but that wasn't the case at all.

Every day working together with my friend for the first couple of months was pretty difficult. We tried our best to be cordial, but it was uncomfortable for both of us. As time went on, things got better and we found that we did in fact work really well together. I also realized that I had been wrong in my judgment of his capabilities.

More importantly, I came to realize that this was one of the most important decisions I ever made, because when I made the choice to deny everything in my flesh that wanted to run as far away as possible and submitted myself to God's plan instead, it opened up the door for incredible growth and prosperity in my life. I had decided to bloom where God had planted me and there's great blessing that comes with that. You decide whether your challenges will define you or refine you. Truthfully, a lot of what's in this book came from what I learned during that season.

When I made the choice to stay in that place, knowing that it was what God had called me to do, I was given more opportunities to bloom than I had in the past. I began personal coaching sessions with a well-known leader in our area, and I met regularly with my pastor to learn from him. I set aside more time to spend with God and to read. I grew more personally and as a leader in that next year than I had in any other year of my life. When I had gone into the interviews with the board of directors I went with an attitude of trying to show how many answers I could offer. Now, I was taking an entirely different approach in learning all that I could.

Blooming began to occur as I significantly improved my public speaking skills based on things my coach identified and taught me. I had been preaching for years, but within months people were regularly complimenting my speaking and pointing out ways they had seen me improve. Instead of shrinking back from this experience, through prayer God began to fill me with a newfound confidence in who I was by affirming and encouraging me to be who He had created me to be.

There was something else that came out of that time. I realized that I didn't have a good hobby. It may sound silly, but when I noticed that I didn't have anything I could do regularly for enjoyment it was like someone had pulled a fire alarm in my brain. This was a warning sign that I wasn't getting the proper rest I needed. When I began looking for a hobby that would interest me, I found the answer was in picking up photography.

I had taken several photography classes in high school and worked at a photo studio when I was in college. I remembered really enjoying being behind the camera, but I hadn't stuck with it because of the cost of buying a really nice camera. Now, years later, I started using my iPhone to find good shots and there were plenty of free apps for editing pictures that made them turn out stunning. I found that photography was a good way to help me slow down and enjoy life, nature and all that God has given me. There were many times when I was out walking and taking photos that God used that time to speak to me.

One summer day I was out taking pictures and stopped to take in the fresh air and sunshine. It was one of those days where the temperature feels perfect. There was a light breeze and the sun felt great as it washed over me. I stopped on a bridge over a small pond in our area as I often do. This is a great spot just to take in the sights and sounds of summer in my tiny town. As I looked around, I saw some dandelion seeds floating in the water and then I noticed there were quite a few floating in the air, too.

As I watched them, I heard God speak to me about how those dandelion seeds appear to float aimlessly with no set course, but when they land they are planted and eventually grow to become a dandelion flower. Any gardener who has to pull these all the time can tell you that dandelions are good at finding a home and quickly spreading to a whole area. Obviously, I don't want to be floating aimlessly without a set course like those dandelions, but I felt like God was saying, "Let me guide you to where I will plant you next. Don't try to make something happen on your own."

In other words, let God plant you and when He does, resolve to bloom in that spot and make the most of it. Here I was. I had just gone through one of the hardest seasons of my life and God was reminding me to trust Him and to be faithful wherever He has placed me.

I'm grateful that there was still a glimmer of hope in my spirit. I think that came from knowing I had heard God's voice and I was doing what He told me to do. I had experienced that same hope at times in my past when I'd been discouraged and trusted His leading and then had seen the proof of His goodness.

As I mentioned before, this was an incredibly challenging time, but it also led to an amazing season of growth in my life. It's funny how storms can do that. Take Death Valley for instance. You may not be aware, but Death Valley is the lowest, driest, and hottest desert in North America. It holds the record for the highest reliably recorded air temperature in the world at 135°F. Deep down I felt like I was in an emotional Death Valley. I felt very low and very dry. At times I felt so discouraged that I wondered when I would feel life come forth again. But did you know that even in a place like Death Valley life can spring up?

In 2016, Death Valley experienced what many call a "super bloom." Even in a place like this, there are occasional flowers that come up, but a super bloom is a magnificent sight to see. More than twenty wildflower species blanket what is normally a dry, lifeless valley floor composed of rocks, soil, and not much else. Park rangers say it is amazing to experience and could be a once-in-a-lifetime opportunity. But the only reason this super bloom occurred in 2016 was because of unusually strong storms and massive amounts of flooding.

Have you ever known someone who faced incredible storms in their life, yet seemed to come through it stronger and closer to God than ever before? While everyone is baffled by the crushing weight of their situation, when they steadily rely on God, the result is a more blessed life than what they had to begin with.

It's amazing how God uses trials in our lives to reveal strengths we never knew lay dormant within us. Death Valley park ranger Alan Van Valkenburg said when the super bloom happened, he realized, "There are so many seeds out there just waiting to sprout, just waiting to grow. I had no idea that there was that much out there."[1]

If you choose to bloom where you're planted, even if it's somewhere that you have no desire to be, I believe God will bless your life and cause it to prosper. There are seeds deep within you that are just waiting to sprout and grow into greater things. There are skills longing to be discovered, character traits waiting to be developed, and victories yearning to be won.

The famous missionary Jim Elliot once said something like, wherever you are, be all there. That's a wonderfully simple thought from a missionary who sacrificed his life for the sake of the Gospel. At twenty-eight years of age, Elliot set out with four other men in 1956 to reach a dangerous tribe in the Ecuador jungle. This tribe was isolated and known for its violence.

After a few friendly encounters with two of the tribesmen, Elliot and the others planned to visit the village, but before they arrived they were attacked by the tribe and all were killed. Several years after his death, his wife and the sister of one of the other men returned to minister to the tribe. The women were welcomed and many of the tribe gave their lives to Christ. If anyone was committed to where God had called them, it was Jim and Elisabeth Elliot. You probably won't be faced with a tragic situation like the Elliots, but the same principle can still apply to where you are. Wherever you are and whatever it is God has called you to, be all there.

So, what does that look like? How do you practically bloom where you're planted? If you can set goals and develop discipline in your life, it will help you grow and

THERE ARE SEEDS DEEP WITHIN YOU THAT ARE JUST WAITING TO SPROUT AND GROW INTO GREATER THINGS.

bloom as a person. The most successful people are usually the most disciplined people. This could look different depending on your situation. In my case, I sought out mentors and coaches, spent more time in prayer, worked diligently at my job every day while honoring my new boss, read more leadership books, and took up photography as a means for relaxation. For you it could mean giving your all at work, being intentional about studying, attending church every week and finding a way to serve, reading your Bible every day, memorizing Scripture, or regularly exercising.

The important thing is to pick a couple of goals and stick with them. Many times we're not good at developing disciplines so don't try to do too much at once. This is one reason why so many people fail to continue New Year's resolutions. Start with something small and work your way up from there. Think of it in the terms of this Chinese proverb, "Every journey begins with the first step." You may want to set one goal and then after a couple of months incorporate another. Scientists have determined that on average it takes over two months of doing an activity for it to become an established habit.[2] Being diligent in your work every day is easier to commit to because going to work is already part of your routine and you quickly earn a paycheck, but when you determine to get up at 6 a.m. to exercise before work, you might begin to wonder if deep down you're a masochist.

The best way to follow through on your goals is by determining your *why?*. If you haven't resolved and written out your reason for why you're going to work at these goals, then they'll become another balled-up piece of paper in that pile of New Year's resolutions. Determining my *why* was the first step in writing this book. When I realized that I could help people walk through their twenties by sharing the things I've experienced and learned, that was the encouragement I needed to follow through with my goals. Once you've determined your *why*, write it down, place it by your bed, and review it each morning before you start your day and every night before you go to sleep.

Most importantly, pray before you set your goals so that you know what you're focusing on is what God has called you to in this season. If you work at something only to find that it wasn't the best thing for right now, you'll end up frustrated. This is the difference between someone who is striving to do something in their own strength and the person who is intentionally choosing to bloom where they're planted. Trust me, I've been on both sides of the fence. But when you know your goals are bigger than yourself because God has given them to you, it will spur you on during days when you don't feel inspired.

Once you've determined your goals and written down your *why's*, then you need to take time to accomplish them. If you incorporate them into your routine, you'll have the greatest chance at seeing success. When I decided to write this book, I knew finding time would be my biggest challenge. I have a busy job that involves traveling and an active family with three small children. I knew I would have to be intentional about my time if I wanted to see this project become a reality. So, I changed my schedule to go to bed earlier and wake up earlier so I would have time to write before my children got up for the day.

All I could find in my schedule was a half hour to devote to writing each day. It was a small start, but it was enough to get me going, and over time I found other small spaces in my schedule where I could do more writing. I have never been a morning person, but knowing my *why* was the thing that helped me pull myself out of bed each morning so I could devote the time needed for this project. There were days it wasn't easy, and there were some days (especially after traveling the night before) that it just didn't happen, but I accomplished far more than I would have had I not taken time for my goals.

Even if you feel as if God has planted you somewhere that you have no desire to be, you can flourish in this time. And, if you can grasp that God wants your life to be full of meaning no matter where you are, then you'll be more likely to find fulfillment. When I was working at the television station, I couldn't see how my life could be meaningful. I worked hard at that job, and even spent hours learning new skills so I could benefit the company, but deep down my attitude toward the organization and some of my coworkers was terrible. I hadn't decided to bloom where I was planted and the result was a regular feeling of dissatisfaction.

Looking back, I realize I would have been much more satisfied if I had maintained a better attitude and asked God to show me how I could bless my coworkers and that company. Eventually, God would lead my wife and me into college ministry where I could see the direct results of what we were doing and how it was impacting lives. In the end, because of God's mercy and grace, He knew what was best for us and led us there, but I still regret that I didn't use my time at that small TV station more effectively. The point is, we are created to have purposeful lives. Our souls crave meaning and wherever you are, you can do something meaningful that will bring growth and contribute to where God plans to take you in the future.

Going back to the story of Jesus and His vineyard, He goes on to say, "If you abide in Me, and My words abide in you, ask whatever you wish, and it will be done for you. My Father is glorified by this, that you bear much fruit, and so prove to be My disciples" (John 15:7-8, NASB). God wants to see us fulfilled in life and bearing much fruit. By staying the course you will reap the rewards. Investment now will pay rewards in the future. If you will plant yourself and be faithful instead of growing impatient and making hasty decisions, you will be blessed. Don't sacrifice your future for your present.

Investing in the stock market is the perfect example of how being patient can lead to big rewards. Financial writer Ben Carlson once described a hypothetical situation he called the unluckiest investor named Bob. Bob made his first investment in the stock market at the beginning of 1973, right before a 48 percent crash for the S&P 500. Bob then held onto stocks after the drop, saving a total of $46,000 more in his savings account, and not getting up

DON'T SACRIFICE YOUR FUTURE FOR YOUR PRESENT.

the nerve to commit more savings until September 1987. That was right before a 34 percent stock market crash. Bob then continued to hold tight, making only two more investments before retirement, which came right before the 2000 crash and then the 2007 crash!

So, how did Bob do after these 42 years of what most would call epic market misfortune? Actually, he made money. Quite a bit of it in fact. Because even though the market crashed after each time he invested, he chose to be patient and not take out his money out of fear. As the market successively made record highs, Bob turned the $184,000 he invested over those 35 years into $1.16 million—for a total profit of $980,000. Because he stayed the course, he reaped great rewards.[3]

It's not always easy to bloom where you're planted and stay the course, especially with the uncertainty that can follow when you graduate college. But if you're willing to trust the Lord and obey Him, it will lead to rewards in your life.

Don't worry. I'm not sharing a "name it and claim it" or "get rich quick" philosophy with you here. In fact, the rewards I'm referring to aren't exclusively finances and there's rarely anything quick about this approach.

As you're faithful in the little, in the times that feel frustrating, and in the times where everything seems like it's up in the air, God will bless your faithfulness. Jesus promised us that when He said, "Whoever can be trusted with very little can also be trusted with much" (Luke 16:10, NIV).

I remember stories my dad shared with me about his experiences after college. He started his journey with very little money and few opportunities. He had graduated with a degree in broadcasting and then went searching for a job. He was struggling to find something in his field, but he was determined to work and earn a living. While going to graduate school to get his MBA, he found himself working back at McDonald's where he had worked throughout high school and during college school breaks.

He was told that ninety percent of students who graduated from the MBA program graduated with a job lined up. The year he graduated, two out of the nineteen students in his class had secured jobs. He decided he wanted to go into the business side of broadcasting, but as he searched for jobs, because he had a master's degree, many employers told him he was overqualified and they feared he wouldn't stick around long enough to make it worth hiring him.

He eventually left McDonald's and, after hearing from the Lord, begrudgingly took a position managing a restaurant. The restaurant had launched just a few months before and within a week he could see that they had made every mistake in the book for starting a new business. He worked ninety-hour work weeks for ten months to try to fix the problems. Then he decided he couldn't continue to bear the stress and the physical toll it was taking on him. When he told the restaurant investors that he was going to look for other work, they closed the restaurant by the end of the week. He was such a hard and caring worker that seeing something he had invested himself into fail like that was a big blow for him.

One of the investors saw how hard a worker he was and decided to hire him for their chimney sweeping business. His position was marketing and advertising the business, but being part of only a two-person operation, he quickly jumped into cleaning chimneys as well. There he was working with an MBA as a chimney sweep. I'm talking straight up Mary Poppins, chim-chim cher-ee style. Unfortunately, he didn't find it quite so glamorous.

But while he was crawling through grease ducts, God's plan for him was coming to fruition. He had taken up an interest in financial planning. This was a fairly new profession at the time and eventually he decided to take the risk, get certifications, and start his own practice.

This is a scary step to take when you've just had your first child, but God had already lined up many of his first clients. They were people he had formed relationships with while doing marketing for the chimney sweep business. Not only had God led him to find his purpose, a career that he is still committed to thirty years later, but He also used this unexpected path to provide the customers that would kickstart it. Some of those people remain his clients to this day.

I'm so grateful my dad shared those stories with me. It took him several years of regularly choosing to bloom where he was planted to figure out what he was going to do with his life. My dad was blessed in that he was able to discover his purpose before he reached thirty. At the age of thirty, I'm still trying to figure some of these things out. But that's exactly what I want you to hear because everyone's story is different. Expecting your timeline to look like someone else's would be like me expecting to be the next Steph Curry every time I set foot on a basketball court. It's good for me to dream, but as a 5' 8" guy with a poor shot and bad dribbling skills, it really doesn't make practical sense.

That's okay, though, because I'm comfortable in knowing that God didn't create me to be the next Steph Curry or the next Adam Levine or the next (insert name here). God created me to be me and you to be you and it's important that you grab hold of that and identify with it. When you begin to walk in your identity in Christ, then you can face the wilderness, find a way to plant yourself, and start to learn what God wants to teach you from it.

CULTIVATE YOUR RELATIONSHIP

I didn't used to consider myself someone who was good at planning things out. I was more likely to make decisions in the moment. And it's not like you have to put a lot of time into deciding, "Do I want to go see a movie tonight?" or "What am I going to have for lunch today?" But when a project is important to me, I'll put a lot of effort into making sure it's a success. It doesn't matter if it takes more of my time and energy, because I know how rewarding it will feel when I see the result of the time I've put in.

When I was in college, I decided it was time to propose to my girlfriend. It's not often that two people start dating in high school and still love each other, let alone like each other, as they near the end of college, but by God's grace Cheryl and I still had both of those going for us. We had been dating for five years and I knew she was the woman I wanted to marry. For me, a marriage proposal was a pretty big deal. Some people keep it simple, but I knew this would be the only time in her life that someone asked her to marry him, and I wanted to make sure it was memorable. The problem was that there were so many ways I could go about setting up the proposal. Just thinking about it almost drove me crazy, and this was before I could just steal the best idea from someone else's proposal on YouTube.

For weeks I agonized over how I wanted to ask her. I tried to think of what could make this different from just any other date. I thought about what things she liked and what would make her feel loved. My mind was spinning for nearly a month as I wrestled with idea after idea. Should I propose in front of a large crowd where tons of people would cheer afterward or would that embarrass her? Should I get her friends and family involved or keep it more of a thing with just the two of us?

After thinking about it for what seemed like forever, my plan slowly started to come together. I decided I would propose at a place in our hometown called the bluffs. These are huge cliffs with a breathtaking view overlooking Lake Ontario. Next, I decided I would set up a table and chairs on top of the bluffs and order a catered dinner. Then I purchased dozens of daffodils, her favorite flower, and scattered them around the table and along a path that led us there. The sunsets over Lake Ontario are incredible, so I planned to propose as the sun was going down.

The big day finally came. I was running everywhere trying to get everything done in time. I wanted everything to be set up perfectly before I went to get her. A situation came up that almost kept us from leaving on time, and

I became more nervous than a kindergartner getting on the bus for the first day of school. At last, I picked her up and we were on our way to the most memorable date we would ever have.

She was so excited when she saw the flowers and even more impressed when she realized I had gotten the meal catered. Later on she told me she had been looking at my pockets to see if I had a ring box in one of them, but she never saw it and decided we must just be having a special date. In hindsight, planning an outdoor date in April in New York may not have been the smartest idea. The temperature dropped as the sun went down and the wind off the lake became increasingly cold. Before I had a chance to pop the big question, she commented that we might need to go before we died from hypothermia.

Then, as the sun was setting, I got down on one knee, pulled out the ring and said, "Well, I do want to spend the rest of my life with you. Will you marry me?" At first she was so surprised; I had caught her so off-guard that she didn't say anything. Her pause felt like such an eternity (it was probably only ten seconds in reality) that I began to hope she hadn't actually developed hypothermia, but finally she said the word I had been waiting to hear all day: "Yes!"

The cold aside, all that time I had spent planning had paid off. Not only did she feel loved, but she could tell she was so important to me that I would go to all this trouble just to be in relationship with her for the rest of our lives. That day was one of the most exciting days of my life.

There was a lot of work that went into it and unexpected challenges that I had to overcome, but it was all worth it in the end.

Unfortunately, a lot of people think that all the work of maintaining a healthy relationship with your significant other is over once you get married. But just marrying my wife wasn't a guarantee of a successful, thriving relationship. Each day requires being intentional so that I can show my wife I love and care for her. I'm purposed in my actions, by doing things like saying good morning when we first wake up, to kissing her before I leave for work, to helping out around the house. I want my relationship with her to be great for the rest of our lives. For that to happen, my relationship with her requires regular thought and action.

Just like I want my relationship with my wife to flourish, I also have seen the value of having a great relationship with God. If you want to have success in life, I mean success in the things that are truly important, you'll need to cultivate your relationship with God. This can be challenging because there are always things begging for our attention. But nothing is more worth your time than your relationship with God.

When you're in college, it's hard to establish routines like Bible reading and prayer. You never go to bed at the same time, your social life changes on the spur of the moment, and when it's midterms or finals, you have to pull all-nighters. Even getting time alone to spend with God is difficult when you have a roommate or can't escape the annoying guy down the hall who thinks he's the resident DJ. But now that you're out of college, you can establish more regular routines.

Routine and *habit* are words that can scare those of us who aren't type A personalities, but we all have established routines and habits whether we realize it or not. Even if you don't plan your every minute, you probably have a pretty similar morning routine that you go through every day. There's an order that you use for showering, eating breakfast, and brushing your teeth. Even when I was in college, my morning routine looked the same most days. I often slept past my alarm, hastily showered and threw on some clothes, then I rushed to make it to class on time. It wasn't a good routine, but it was a routine nonetheless.

Establishing a routine is important because it helps you prioritize your time. I've met many people who truly want to have a quiet time (time spent reading their Bible and praying) each day, but they never find time to make it work. They have good hearts, just not good priorities. Good intentions are much different than good actions. Just as I had to be intentional to pull off an elaborate proposal, if you want to start forming good habits and routines, you'll need to be intentional about it.

The secret to being intentional is not really that big a secret; it starts with caring. Have you ever noticed that when you get a new car, it suddenly seems like everyone around you has the same model? You never noticed it before, but now you see it everywhere on the road. Did everyone else hear you got that car and decide to follow suit so they could be trendy like you? No, they've been driving that car for awhile now, but because it's something you care about, it has become something you notice. As self-centered as it is, humans naturally pay attention to the things they care about.

In the same way, you won't put time into developing a relationship with God if you don't care about it. King David of the Bible knew this to be true. David was known as someone who was close to God. He was known as someone who spent time in God's presence regularly and yet this is what he said in one of the psalms, "O God, you are my God; earnestly I seek you; my soul thirsts for you; my flesh faints for you, as in a dry and weary land where there is no water" (Psalm 63:1, ESV).

You see, David had discovered that to be close to God you have to be consistently taking time to seek Him. He cared about being close to God because he knew it was the most important aspect of his life. It was because of his relationship with God that he was protected when King Saul tried to kill him multiple times. It was because of his relationship with God that he was chosen to be the next king of Israel. God desires a close relationship with you, but to be close to Him, you have to be intentional in looking for ways to spend time with Him.

When you gave your life to the Lord, you began a relationship. But that's exactly what it was – a beginning. If you decide not to build on, not to foster that beginning relationship, then you will find yourself completely unsatisfied as a Christian. You'll be looking around thinking, I thought they told me there was more to this. I thought they told me Christianity was the answer. Am I still missing out? And the answer is Yes, you are. You are missing out because you've neglected to keep working on the relationship that you began with God.

Anyone can start a marriage, but it takes work to keep one going. Anyone can start a relationship, but few are successful at keeping them. It's just like starting a new friendship or the way you approach your college career. It's easy to begin those things. It's easy to meet someone new or fill out a college application, but then comes the part that requires more effort. You have to actually work to keep that relationship going and develop it. You have to work at studying and go to class to stay in college.

But you're willing to do those things when it's important to you. It's important that you stay in touch with good friends, it's important that you finish college and get a degree.

For me, it was crucial that I made sure to propose in a way that made my wife Cheryl feel loved and valued. And if your relationship with God is important, it will directly reflect in how much time you invest into it. But here's the good news. Even if you haven't always done great at cultivating a relationship with God, you can start any time.

Look, if you haven't been investing time into your relationship with God, He isn't upset with you for that, but rather He's thinking to Himself, I really love spending time with you. I want you to get to know Me more. And it's when you take that time to seek Him that you will then experience how incredible living the Christian life can be.

One evening I was walking around the yard outside the apartment building we live in. I began to notice the angle the sun was at and how beautifully it was illuminating everything around. As someone who enjoys photography, I tend to look for moments to capture on my phone even if I'm just taking out the trash.

As I studied this sunset, I saw something else, too. The field in front of the setting sun was covered with dandelions. Normally dandelions aren't very appealing to me. Usually they look fairly boring, but tonight, with the way the sun was falling on them, they looked different. They actually looked beautiful. I bent down low to capture the sunlight hitting one of the dandelions and as I did, I am certain I heard God whisper something in my ear. What I heard left me contemplating the words for hours. He said, "Anything can be beautiful if given the right attention."

I believe that statement can apply to so many different aspects of life, but it is especially meaningful as we consider our relationship with God. If we're being honest, most of us probably feel as if we could have a better relationship with God. And if what God told me in that moment is true, then there is hope that our relationship with Him can be beautiful if given the right attention. Just like a plant needs the right attention to grow successfully, our relationship with God needs the right attention if we are to see it thrive. There are three main ways to do this – talking to Him in prayer, reading the Bible, and spending time in worship.

In his book, *God Has Spoken*, famous theologian J.I. Packer writes, "God's friendship with men and women begins and grows through speech. His to us in revelation, and ours to Him in prayer and praise. Though I cannot see God, He and I can yet be personal friends, because in revelation He talks to me."[1] The revelation he's referring to here is how God reveals Himself to us through the Bible and how we can hear God speak to us in prayer.

Prayer is simply talking to and listening to God. It is a conversation. In our lives, prayer is the grease that makes the engine go. Going throughout life without prayer is like driving a car without putting oil in the engine. You won't get nearly as far as you could. It may feel strange at first, but it's an opportunity to be honest with God and open your heart to Him. This takes practice, but just like with my wife, our relationship would not benefit if there were things she didn't know about me. Prayer is an incredibly powerful way to connect with God. The Bible tells us, "The prayer of a righteous person is powerful and effective" (James 5:16, NIV). Making space in your routine for a daily prayer time is really important and beneficial. Start with a reasonable goal like praying for five minutes and then you can always increase the amount of time once you've gotten into a successful routine.

I would suggest picking a time that you're normally alert and don't have many other commitments. Think about a time you would normally spend mindlessly scrolling through social media or watching a TV show. Then put your phone on Do Not Disturb so you're not distracted. If you're really having trouble remembering to do it, put a daily reminder in your phone or determine that you won't do something else you would never skip (like showering or eating dinner) until you've done your prayer time.

As you actively spend more time in prayer, eventually you can learn to hear God's voice. Now, I know my wife's voice so well that I don't need to look at caller ID when she calls; when I hear her voice I know that it's her. And over time you'll begin to know the voice of God through prayer. It's very rare that someone hears the voice of God in an audible way, but it can happen. Usually it sounds more like a thought within your head.

Often you'll find yourself questioning if what you just heard was your own thought or God speaking. It takes time to determine which it is, but it's helpful that God has given us the Bible to help us test what we're hearing and determine if it's from God or not. Anything that we think may be the voice of God must first align with what the Scriptures say. This is why it's important to be reading and studying the Bible regularly so that you can go back and determine if something you're hearing makes sense with what God's Word says.

Throughout this book there will be various times I talk about hearing God's voice, as I did above with the dandelion. It's taken years of seeking God in prayer and through reading the Bible for me to clearly understand when I'm hearing God's voice and when I'm just thinking my own thoughts. There are still times that I don't always get it right, but for the most part I've learned to distinguish between the two. It's not easy to explain in a five-step process, but it is worth the time and effort to get to know God's voice.

You can grow in determining God's voice through regular practice. Set aside time to be still, focus on Him, and wait to hear His voice. In a world where we're used to filling every free moment by looking at Facebook or playing a game on our phones (guilty as charged), this will be incredibly difficult at first. But, over time you can train your mind to focus and be quiet. Tell God that you're coming to Him because you want to hear His voice. This is what King David was doing when he said, "Earnestly I seek You" (Psalm 63:1, ESV). And God will be so delighted when you do this because He longs to spend time with you.

Praying with a friend can also help you practice hearing God's voice. I have a friend whom I regularly pray with, and when we pray, we take the majority of our time to listen for God's voice and then we share with each other what we heard. Sometimes we spend half an hour or more on the phone just listening for God to speak. This probably sounds strange to you, but I've found that this practice has really helped me learn to hear God's voice better. There are many times that God gives us words to share with one another.

Over the years I've shared words with him that have most likely been my thoughts more than God's words, and

I'm sure he could say the same. As we've continued to lean into God and listen for His voice, though, we've gotten better at discerning when it's Him speaking and when it's just us. As the years have gone by, we've seen words that we've given each other come to pass. When you see that happen, then you can confidently say you've heard God's voice and it strengthens your desire even more to keep listening for what He wants to say to you.

Even though there have been times I've gotten it wrong, I don't give up listening because I want to be someone who hears God. This is not something to take lightly. We have to be very careful with any word we share with others that we believe God has given us because our words are incredibly powerful and can have a big influence in the lives of others. When you want to grow in hearing God's voice, it is best practice to submit what you're hearing to leaders in your life. Ask them what they think before you take it to heart or share it with another person. And remember that the Bible says anything God speaks to us for sharing with others will be for strengthening, encouragement, and comfort (1 Corinthians 14:3, NIV). If it doesn't fit in one of those categories, it isn't God.

Reading the Bible is another way that we can hear God's voice. The Bible is called the Word of God because it is the words He has spoken and things He has done over time that have been written down and recorded. God gave us His word so we can have a healthy relationship with Him. The Bible expresses how much God loves us. He loves us so much that He would leave His written Word with us so we can continue to connect with Him. He's done His part to reach out to us, but we must in turn reach out to Him. He wants to be in relationship with us, and we have an amazing opportunity to know the same God who formed the universe by opening up the Word.

There are so many ways to read the Bible, but if you're just starting out, using a Bible reading plan is great. There are many available and they're easy to find online or by downloading the YouVersion Bible app. You can also read free commentaries online that help explain the parts of the Bible that are confusing.

When you study a subject in school, if there's something you don't understand, then you do a little research to make sense of it. But often we don't think to apply the same process to the Bible even though it was written from the perspective of people in a completely different time and culture.

By looking to understand what you're reading and setting aside the time to get into the Word, you'll be amazed at the ways God reveals Himself to you through the scriptures.

The third way we can connect with God is in worship. I often think of worship as sitting in a church service or my bedroom singing along to songs. You can engage in worship that way, but worship is more than that. Worship is thanking God and reflecting on the things He's done in your life. It's also a great way to refocus your mind, especially when you're feeling stressed and are more likely to lose sight of all that God has done. I find worship to be incredibly helpful when I've had a tough day at work or gotten frustrated by my children acting up.

Try starting your day by thanking Him for all He's done and for giving you another day to live for Him. You could do this before you get out of bed or when you first jump in the shower. Then look for other opportunities to worship Him throughout the day by listening to worship music in the car, while getting in a run, or while working. The main concept here is finding ways to keep your mind centered on Him. There's no way you'll be able to do this every moment of every day. In fact, if you can do it ten percent of the day you'll be doing well. But it's not about numbers and minutes spent, it's about making it a priority to develop a relationship with your heavenly Father.

I want you to experience the joy of knowing God more intimately. I want you to experience the satisfaction and peace that comes from having a relationship with Him. But don't get too strict about it. This isn't supposed to be a burden or a chore; it's meant to be something that blesses you and God. If I decide that I want to show my wife I love her by making sure to kiss her every day at exactly 3 p.m., I'm going to stress myself out. I'll either lose track of time or it will be 2:59 and I'll be thinking I have to leave work and get home right now to make sure I kiss her at exactly 3 p.m.!

Not only will it stress me out and make it feel like a chore, but most likely my wife won't feel loved either because love is something that should flow out of us. We should have a desire to love and serve God. It won't come easily every day, but if we're looking to spend time with Him our hearts will follow. There are all these things that compete for our time – video games, hanging out with friends, watching tv, going to the movies, and studying. They're not bad things. I really enjoy playing video games and hanging out with friends myself, but there are good things and then there are great things. I want to spend my time on great things.

You and I make choices about how we spend our time every day. Every day I choose either to pay attention to my relationship with my wife and work on it, or to ignore it. Every day I choose to spend time with God or ignore Him. You have a choice to make about how you're going to spend your time today. Is it going to be spent on things that won't last or on building your relationship with God? Nothing is more worth your time than your relationship with God.

When you regularly give your time to read the Bible, pray, and worship God, you'll experience what David did. David discovered that spending time with God was the greatest thing he could do in life. In fact, he considered it even better than life itself when he wrote, "Your unfailing love is better than life itself; how I praise You! I will praise you as long as I live, lifting up my hands to you in prayer. You satisfy me more than the richest feast. I will praise you with songs of joy" (Psalm 63:3-5, NLT).

Even though I've talked about the effort it takes to keep this relationship going by being intentional and spending time with God each day, I find one way I do that is through constantly remembering all God has done in my life. When I'm thanking Him regularly for what He's done, it's much easier for me to want to spend time with Him. The sacrifice that He made for me when Jesus died on the cross is so great that I don't want to ever take it for granted. Just like I wanted Cheryl to feel loved and valued when I proposed, I always want God to know that I love and value my relationship with Him.

That's why I wrote earlier about establishing routine and habits. Sure, your life will never allow for routine all the time. There will be busy seasons at work, vacations, or possibly babies to keep you up at night. However, the better you are at establishing routines, the better you'll be at prioritizing spending time with God and cultivating your relationship with Him.

Every morning my wife wakes up early so she can get in some exercise before our children awake, pulling at her legs and making messes for her to clean up (another form of exercise she gets). She's exercised faithfully for many years, even before we had children. I must admit that I do not share the same passion and commitment to exercise that she does. I tried for several months to wake up with her to exercise, but I found working out in the morning to be about as enjoyable as putting my arm in a meat grinder. I'm really good at establishing other habits though, like making sure I get three full meals in every day.

Seriously though, I admire my wife's commitment to work out. She's not one of those crazy people who actually enjoys exercise (if that's you, I said it, you're crazy) and she has had times where she was too sick, pregnant, or just plain tired to get out of bed and do it, but for the most part she has established a routine and held to it for years. That's quite impressive. But it's because she has seen the value of being healthy, made it a priority, and then formed a routine that she has been able to stick with.

You can also establish healthy routines if you see the value in it. Remember what I wrote earlier – anything can be beautiful if given the right attention. Just like my desire to bless my future wife with a grand proposal, routines must come from a heart of love for God. I promise that if you resolve to develop your relationship with God, you won't regret it. I can say that with confidence because the Bible gives us this promise. In fact, King David wrote about it in another one of the psalms, "Taste and see that the Lord is good; blessed is the one who takes refuge in Him" (Psalm 34:8, NIV).

When we spend time developing a relationship with God, it leads to blessing and gives us a place of refuge. We can get so caught up in looking at our lives and thinking *If I'm not careful I'm going to miss it!* Fill in whatever the "it" is for you: the right job, your future spouse, God's direction for your life, etc. You're right, if you're not careful you will miss it. But the "it" isn't what you think it is. The "it" that you must make sure you don't miss is actually your relationship with God. Nothing is more worth your time than your relationship with God.

NOTHING IS MORE WORTH YOUR TIME THAN YOUR RELATIONSHIP WITH GOD.

#WHATSNEXTBOOK

YOU DON'T HAVE TO WORRY ABOUT WHO YOU ARE (OR ARE NOT)

Were you a dork when you were younger? I was. In fact, I still am to an extent. I hate to admit it, but I understand almost all the jokes when I watch an episode of "The Big Bang Theory." I attended a Christian school and even with a dress code, where everyone is pretty much wearing the same thing, you can still be geeky. The school's dress code was khaki pants and a polo shirt or sweater. It should have been easy to blend in. I love my mom very much and she did a great job of raising three boys, but kid's fashion just wasn't one of her strengths. She would buy pants that were too short and had elastic in the waistbands and legs that caused the pants to bunch up and look ridiculous.

Then there were the sweaters. I'm talking rainbow-colored, geometric patterns. I was looking back at school pictures and my mom must have really liked one of those sweaters because she had me wear it three years in a row for class picture day! Remember that song that says, "I wish that I could be like the cool kids?" That could have been my anthem all throughout primary and middle school.

I remember one day during middle school when I was sitting around the lunch table with my classmates. Being a private school, our class was pretty small, so everyone was involved in the conversation. As we were talking, I saw an opportunity to make a joke at someone else's expense. This was the kind of joke that the cool kids had made about me plenty of times. I jumped in and hit them with the one-liner. If anyone else had said it, the group would have roared with laughter, but because I was the dork something strange happened.

In a moment of unusual mercy (at least for the kid I had picked on), the cool kids began to turn against me. One of them said, "Chris, why would you say that? That's such a mean thing to joke about." I could feel my cheeks turning red with embarrassment and suddenly I felt two inches tall. Looking back on that, I can see that I tried to be someone I'm not. I wasn't a mean kid, and I wasn't someone who normally made jokes at the expense of others. But I wanted so bad to be cool that I was trying to make up for my insecurities and gain the approval of my classmates. It backfired.

While I've had to struggle with my insecurities and find ways to overcome them, I know I'm not the only one. Even major celebrities battle insecurities. Actor Ryan Gosling said in an interview once, "I'm not that good looking. I think I'm a pretty weird-looking guy."[1] Robert Pattinson shared that he is more insecure since the success of the *Twilight* movies. He said, "You have to confront your insecurities quite a lot, and I have plenty, plenty of insecurities. Even more now."

Anna Kendrick from *Pitch Perfect* said, "I get insecure about everything. I'm still bewildered when people know my name or my face." And Jessica Alba recounting her time in school gave this description of herself, "I was pigeon-toed, had a sway back, was slightly cross-eyed, buck-toothed, and sucked my thumb."[2] That's enough to make anyone feel insecure!

We all have insecurities, even people who seem like they have it all together. Let me quickly define what I mean by insecurities. An insecurity is an uncertainty or anxiety about oneself. It's a lack of confidence. Another way to put it is that insecurity is the gap between what you think you are and what you want to be.

If not dealt with, insecurities will affect every area of your life: your relationship with Christ, your relationships with others, even the things you will aspire to and ultimately achieve. Would you be surprised to hear that self-doubt can be the biggest thing that cripples you and holds you back from living out your God-given purpose? Think about that for a moment. More than education, career choices, or even money, the number one thing that can hold you back is your insecurities.

When I was passed up for the executive director position that I mentioned in the last chapter, all my insecurities suddenly wanted to rise to the surface. Lies others had told me or I had believed about myself for years quickly became the loudest voices clamoring for attention over my other thoughts. It was in prayer that God spoke something so valuable to me, "Chris, your validation should not come from man. It should only come from me and you have My approval." It's so easy to think we're the only one who struggles with insecurity, but everyone fights this battle in one way or another.

In actuality, insecurity has been around since nearly the beginning of time. We can see it as far back as the Garden of Eden as I'll discuss in a minute, but you can go even further back to see it at work when the position of Satan was birthed through insecurity.

Before Satan's downfall, he was an angel who was the chief worship leader in heaven. Eventually, he became jealous of all the worship God was getting and wanted some for himself. He wasn't secure in his role and his insecurity caused his demise. Not content to be miserable all by himself, he came to Eve in the garden to see if he could rope her into joining him.

When Satan comes to Eve, the first thing he says to her is, "Indeed, has God said, 'You shall not eat from any tree of the garden'?" (Genesis 3:1, NASB). Now, of course, this question wasn't even close to true. God had given Adam and Eve dominion over the entire garden. Satan made it sound like they weren't able to eat from any tree, when the truth was that God had told them there was only one they couldn't partake of. This was a trick in an attempt to encourage Eve to start doubting God's goodness and it worked. She began to doubt if what God wanted was best for her. She didn't trust His reason for withholding access to just one little tree was because He cared about her.

So, in taking the fruit and eating it, Adam and Eve exchanged the belief that God had only good things for them into the belief that He was hiding something from them. When Eve stopped believing that God is always good, she no longer saw herself as a daughter of the Creator of the universe who had been given every good thing. Instead, she saw herself as someone who was missing out on something. What happened in that moment forever changed humankind, and it's crucial for us to remember when we battle our own insecurities because, like Eve, when we don't stand on who God is, we lose sight of who we are.

Let's return to Moses for a minute. When Moses encountered the burning bush, he started to make the same mistake and it almost stopped him from going to Egypt and rescuing God's chosen people. Here he was, faced with a burning bush that was talking to him and wouldn't burn up, and yet he questioned his qualifications. When God gave Moses the instructions to go to Egypt, his first response was, "Who am I that I should go to Pharaoh and bring the Israelites out of Egypt?" (Exodus 3:11, NIV). Moses was facing the Almighty God in a burning bush, getting to speak to Him directly, and yet he questions himself, saying, "Who am I?" Maybe you've had times in your life where you ask yourself the same question, "Who

WHEN WE DON'T STAND ON WHO GOD IS, WE LOSE SIGHT OF WHO WE ARE.

am I? And what do I have to offer?" But you don't have to worry about who you are or are not, when you trust in who God is.

Moses went on to ask God, "Suppose I go to the Israelites and say to them, 'The God of your fathers has sent me to you,' and they ask me, 'What is his name?' Then what shall I tell them?" (Exodus 3:13, NIV). And this is when God replies and tells him to say that "I AM" sent him. God was communicating to Moses that He is the utmost source of life. Everything we see and experience begins and ends with Him. While that should have been a sufficient answer for Moses, it wasn't enough for him to trust in who God is and stand firm on that. He made the same mistake as Eve. When he chose not to stand on who God is, Moses lost sight of who he was.

When Adam and Eve allowed their insecurities to have power over them, they became powerless. The Bible tells us they realized they were naked and hid themselves from the presence of the Lord God in the garden. Up until this point, they had been given dominion over the entire earth. Their job was to take care of the wonderful place God had created. But in a moment, they went from having power over all the earth and animals to hiding naked among the trees in the garden.

Eve didn't even get what she wanted or was promised by Satan. She believed a lie and it brought her to a place where she was completely powerless. They had become powerless against sin, powerless as people, and powerless to carry out the calling God had given them. And when we believe the lies our insecurities tell us, we are powerless to stop them from wreaking havoc on ourselves and those around us.

I remember a time when my insecurities overtook me, and I was powerless to stop them. I was talking with a friend of mine who was sharing about how she had recently gotten back into running. She was a mom of three and was excited to be getting some exercise and making progress in her goals. She talked about how after a lot of hard work she had gotten to the point of running a 5K in thirty-two minutes. Without thinking much about it, I began to brag saying something to the effect of, "Yeah, I hardly ever run but when I do I can run a 5K in about thirty minutes."

Almost immediately I could see the hurt in her eyes from that statement. In just a moment, I had taken all that hard work she had done and made her feel like she hadn't accomplished anything. I realized afterwards how stupid that was and how ridiculous I had been. I'm actually really ashamed to share this story with you. But the point is that I so badly wanted to feel good about myself, to feel like I was cool, that I had no regard for my friend and her feelings in that moment. I just said it so quickly that I didn't even give myself a chance to evaluate what I was thinking before I said it. I had given my insecurities power over me, and I was powerless to stop them.

I wish I could tell you that I did the right thing and went back and apologized, but sadly I couldn't bring myself to do it and the moment passed. I've since asked

God to forgive me and worked a lot to make sure I'm aware of my insecurities and to avoid letting them have power over me. Overcoming our insecurities isn't always easy and often God has to continue reminding us of who He is and who He created us to be.

In the story of Moses, God goes on to tell him that the elders of Israel will listen to him, tells him about plans to perform wonders through him, and even concludes by saying that the Egyptians will give the Israelites their silver, gold, and clothing when they leave Egypt. But Moses isn't satisfied. He still isn't convinced that he is best for this assignment and continues to question the Lord. He questions what he will do if the Israelites don't believe him and tells God that he can't speak well. Throughout this exchange, God continues to assure Moses that He hasn't made a mistake by choosing him. God has an answer for every excuse Moses comes up with. At every point in this conversation, God shows Moses that He is more than sufficient to make up for all of his insufficiencies because God was the only one who could bridge the gap between who Moses thought he was and who he wanted to be.

When Moses questions what he will do if the Israelites don't believe him, God shows him how he will use his staff to perform miracles. When Moses complains that he can't speak well, God says, "Who gave human beings their mouths? Who makes them deaf or mute? Who gives them sight or makes them blind? Is it not I, the Lord? Now go; I will help you speak and will teach you what to say" (Exodus 4:11-12, NIV). Can you believe that this wasn't enough to convince Moses? Moses was so focused on his insecurities and feeling unqualified that he forgot who God was.

When Moses continues to persist and requests that God send someone else, the Bible says that the Lord's anger burned against him. Finally, God offers Moses the option of having his brother, Aaron, speak on his behalf, and it's then that Moses gives in and agrees to go back to Egypt. It's amazing to me that Moses had so much trouble taking God at His word. It's almost incomprehensible that he could be given a task directly from the God who created the entire universe, laid out before him clear as day, and still feel unqualified to carry it out. It's hard to believe, until I realize that I do the same thing all the time.

There are so many times in life that I have felt insufficient to carry out the things God has called me to. When my wife and I decided to leave steady jobs behind to raise funds as missionaries, we felt unsure of how we would effectively do that. When my boss asked me to take on the role of assistant director, I was excited, but at the same time in awe that God would give me such responsibility. When my first child was born, I worried about being an adequate father. And when God called me to write this book, I questioned if I was good enough and had enough to offer for this project to sufficiently help others. But, time after time, when I've felt as if I was a nobody who didn't have much to offer, God has assured me that He is more than sufficient to cover all of my insufficiencies.

A few years back, our local church hosted a guest speaker named Dr. Mike Brown. There were several special services and on the night of the last meeting he gave an altar call. I don't remember what the altar call was for, but God was moving on my heart and I responded. At that point in my life I had been asking God for answers to some questions and had a strong desire to accomplish more for Him, but felt unsure about myself. As I was standing at the altar that night, Dr. Mike Brown paced back and forth on stage and began to pray for us as a group; suddenly, he stopped in his tracks, pointed at me, and said something that I remember clearly to this day. He looked me right in the eyes and said, "You can stand before presidents and kings." Then he went back to praying for the group.

I don't share this story with you to brag in any way. I'm not sure that I will stand before presidents and kings, although I have more faith for it now than I ever did before. I just know that in that moment God showed me how He sees me, and I realized that it's much different from how I see myself. For all of my insecurities and feelings of insufficiency, God sees incredible potential in me. And being that He planned out my days before I was even in the womb, I've decided that I'm going to trust what He says about me instead of what I think about me.

God sees you in ways that you could never see yourself. Moses saw himself as someone who was totally unqualified and yet, God chose him because He knew that Moses was the one He wanted to use to free his people from slavery. We are created in God's image; thus it stands to reason that we can do great things with our lives. How often do we lose sight of that truth and let our insecurities dictate who we are and what we can do?

When you question yourself, you question if God is good. When you question if you're too fat, too skinny, too ugly, too awkward, too dorky, or too inadequate, when you question if you're good enough, if you're likable, if you're someone who's worth other people's time, you're saying to the Creator of the universe – you got it wrong! God didn't mess up when He created you. He did not get it wrong.

Things may have happened to you that He never intended, things that have impacted you in negative ways and caused doubt and insecurity to enter your life. But the person that He originally made you to be is still in there, and He created you with great things in mind. What God spoke to Jeremiah still rings true today, "For I know the plans I have for you ... plans to prosper you and not to harm you, plans to give you hope and a future" (Jeremiah 29:11, NIV).

Last summer I decided to take a personal day to spend in prayer and reflection. I wanted to get away from everything else for a little bit and hear what God was saying for this season. I had heard about a monastery nearby where anyone can go and spend time in complete silence.

Now, before you go thinking I'm all crunchy, hear me out. Just two years ago I would have thought I was crazy too. But I heard about this quiet place from my pastor who's a pretty solid guy and, as far as I know, he's never backpacked across country eating only Clif bars and sleeping in lean-tos.

So, I decided to give it a try. I got there early in the morning and spoke with a monk who directed me to one of the houses used for guests. The house was eerily quiet when I entered, but, after all, that's what I had come for. I made my way through the first floor to determine what I should do next. I found a couple of people in the kitchen who had apparently stayed the night and were now eating breakfast in silence, of course. I knew I needed to figure out what the protocols were for getting a room, but having never visited a speechless monastery before, I wasn't sure of the best way to go about doing that. I looked around hoping to find some kind of clue as to what I should do. Nothing, that I could see. Should I use sign language or Jedi mind tricks to communicate with the breakfast guests? For crying out loud, why didn't I think to ask the monk whom I had spoken with earlier? I thought to myself.

After a minute or so that felt like an awkward eternity, I approached one of the men and whispered in the most hushed tone I could manage, "I'm looking to get a room. What should I do?" Thankfully, he was happy to oblige. He led me over to a board on the wall where you could see available rooms and sign in. There he showed me a list of rules and explained in hushed tones what I should do. I signed up for an unoccupied room and wandered back down the hallway to find what would be my sanctuary for the next couple of hours.

I opened the door marked #6 to see that it was the size of a small walk-in closet with minimal decoration. There was a twin bed with linens, accompanied by a battery-operated clock and small desk with chair. In the corner beside the door was a modest private bathroom. I hadn't been expecting much, so this certainly would suffice. I began to unload the backpack I had brought with my Bible, notebook, some other reading material and headphones, just in case I got to the point where I couldn't stand the silence any longer.

I spent the next couple of hours in prayer, reading the Bible and then eventually got into a book I had brought along called *Start.* by Jon Acuff. As I read, I came across a chapter talking about our internal voices. Acuff wrote that none of us has a positive internal voice. He says that our internal voices will always try to discourage and derail us from accomplishing the things we're called to do. He encouraged the reader to write down a list of what their internal voices were saying and then in a corresponding column beside that to write down what is really true.

As I wrote down these lies I believe from my internal voice and then the contrary truths, it turned out to be a powerful exercise for me. I would encourage you to do the same. There are things we tell ourselves all the time because we've given our insecurities power over us. And when you begin to determine what they are and why you believe them, they begin to lose their power.

The first lie I tell myself that I wrote down is, "I'm not good enough." Whether it's at writing, speaking, parenting, whatever it is, I often believe that I'm not good enough at it. In the corresponding column I wrote down the truth, "God says I am more than good enough. He created me perfect." By writing that down I wasn't trying to downplay the fact that I can always learn and grow in areas, but I know I'm good at remembering I need to do those things. I know that I often forget that God has created me more than good enough and equipped me to do the things He's called me to do. So, I wrote down what was most important for me to remember when I begin to believe this lie.

The second lie I wrote down was, "I'll never be as good at _____ as _____." I can fill in the blanks in multiple areas as I struggle with this one regularly. So, in the truth column I wrote, "Why do I have to? I don't. Being who God created me to be instead of comparing myself to others and trying to imitate them will always be better." In all, I wrote down five lies and truths during that time, but I'm sure I could have come up with many more. Over the last year this has become a powerful tool for me. Now when I find I'm telling myself these lies I can go back to my notebook and remind myself of what God has said about me and what the truth really is. It's actually become second nature for me so that now I don't even have to look at my notebook. I just rehearse the truths in my mind from memory.

Remember, confronting your insecurities and declaring the truth over your life is vitally important because it releases you to live to your full potential. Your ability to accomplish the purpose God has given you will be hindered until you can get past your insecurities. So, when your insecurities try to tell you who to be, you need to declare who God is and what He says about you. In His Word we are called sons and daughters, His chosen ones, and the redeemed. Remember, you are so valuable to Him that He gave His only son, Jesus, to rescue you. When you stand on that truth you don't have to live with the lies of insecurity that cause you to doubt who you are and your significance.

Often our insecurities lead us to compare ourselves with others. This was one of the main lies I identified during that exercise. When Moses started comparing himself to others, saying he was slow of speech and that he wasn't the right man for the job, it caused God to get angry with him. Moses' issues with comparison actually led to his brother Aaron getting involved in the mission Moses had been given because God gave in to Moses' complaints. Aaron's involvement would later cause big problems for Moses when he let the people create the golden calf and worship it. If Moses had been able to recognize that God saw him as perfectly qualified even when he saw himself as completely unqualified, he could have avoided a lot of trouble.

Maybe you've heard the phrase before: "God doesn't call the qualified, he qualifies the called." Comparison is a pointless activity because God purposely didn't create us to be like anyone else. Don't compare yourself to others. God created you unique because He wants to do something unique through you. You have so much to contribute by being who you are. God created you and gave you unique giftings so that you would reach the world with them. You have so much bound up potential that is just waiting to come out if you would let go and trust in who God is and who He's made you to be.

God is more than sufficient to cover all of your insufficiencies.

When I was in my early teens, my dad decided to take my brother and me on a canoe trip along with my grandfather. My dad was an Eagle Scout, but he had never really passed on the whole love for the outdoors to us. We weren't big campers, having only gone once or twice as a family, but he remembered doing something like this with his dad as a kid and wanted to recreate the experience. We planned to canoe out to an island, set up a couple of tents, catch some large bass, and cook our meals over an open fire like real men do. My brother and I were flying high with excitement as we packed the car. We would cook s'mores, talk about sports, and explore the unknown island. It was just the kind of adventure little boy dreams are made of.

My grandfather had a large canoe they had used when my dad was younger, but it wouldn't be enough to hold all we needed. So, my dad had arranged to borrow another large canoe from a client of his. We strapped the two canoes onto the cars, making sure they were secure, and commenced on our journey. It would take about two hours to get to our final destination. As we set

GOD IS MORE THAN SUFFICIENT TO COVER ALL OF YOUR INSUFFICIENCIES.

off, we quickly realized there was one thing we hadn't anticipated that day. It seemed like a storm was blowing in with incredibly strong winds. You might have an idea where this is going.

We only got about ten minutes down the road before we heard a sound you never want to hear when you've got a canoe on top of your car. Have you ever seen a canoe fly? Well, we looked out the window of my dad's SUV to see just that. The canoe my dad had borrowed from his client flipped through the air and landed in a field beside the road.

We pulled the car over as fast as we could, jumped out, and raced over to the canoe, anticipating the worst. Luckily, the canoe was quite strong and had only incurred a few dents and dings. So, we hoisted it back onto the roof, making sure to secure it even tighter than before and again we were off.

The wind gusts kept coming and each time the canoe slid abruptly from side to side we stopped to make sure it wasn't going anywhere. We made it another half hour or so before we heard that awful sound again and saw the same terrible sight. We rushed to the side of the canoe thankful to see that, while it had suffered more dents, the overall structure was still intact. As we lifted it back onto my dad's Ford Expedition, we tried our best to determine why the other canoe on my grandpa's car had not really moved. The only thing we could guess was that his car was lower to the ground and so the winds weren't able to get under the canoe as much.

So, hoping we had found the best way to secure the canoe once and for all, we continued on our trip. We were determined to discover all that the unknown island had to offer. My dad decided to slow our speed in an effort to preserve the canoe, and we trudged on in what had become a much longer journey than expected. This time the canoe stayed in place longer, although we still had to stop every now and then to check our tie downs. It wasn't until we were about half an hour from our destination that we again heard that frightful noise and witnessed the dreadful sight of a twelve-foot-long canoe toppling through the air. This time we approached the boat to see that it had met its fate. One of the main support beams had been split in half.

Now we had a decision to make. Had we come this far only to turn around and possibly expose the canoe to more damage on the long drive home? Or should we finish what we started and hope there would be less wind when we drove home in a couple of days? One thing I should mention about Zeiglers is that we can be pretty stubborn at times. So, we refused to give in and forged ahead. A short time later we pulled into where we would leave our cars and breathed a collective sigh of relief.

I wish I could tell you that this story ends well. I wish I could say that during those next few days spent on the island, we felt like Tom Sawyer and Huckleberry Finn as we reeled in enormous bass under beautiful sunsets and explored mysterious caves. Unfortunately, that wasn't the case. Don't worry, though, the canoe wasn't so badly damaged that anyone drowned. But the first night was practically sleepless as the winds howled and tore at the sides of our tents. The next morning we set out to fish, only to catch a few small rainbow trout that weren't worth keeping. In the end, the best thing I got out of the outing was this story that we now laugh about over holiday dinners as we bemoan our famous canoe trip.

Looking back, we still aren't sure why the canoe on my grandfather's car stayed secure while the one borrowed from my dad's client kept tumbling off. The two were similar in shape, size, and build, yet when the winds came the borrowed canoe couldn't stay secure. It didn't matter what we did, it was not going to stay on the car. The difference was that the wind was able to get under one and throw it off course and damage it while the other stayed secure. In the end, the borrowed canoe was pretty broken. It was still functional, but it wasn't as good as it was when it was first made.

You and I can be just like that canoe that wouldn't stay secure. We start down the road of life made to function a certain way. But when someone hurls an insult at us or we believe something that's not true, the wind comes and throws us off course. We get a little bent out of shape, but overall the damage isn't too bad, so we pick ourselves up and continue on toward our goals. As we continue, something else catches us by surprise or things that happened to us in the past bring out our insecurities again. This time we're more damaged, but not yet entirely broken. If we don't deal with our insecurities, they can hurt us or those around us. And while we see ourselves as the ones being tossed about, God looks at us and says, "If you'd only trust in me and who I created you to be, I will keep you secure, unaffected by the winds that come against you." He is more than sufficient to cover all of your insufficiencies.

Maybe at times you've questioned if you really have anything to offer. Maybe you've wondered if you're where God wants you to be or if you're walking in His will for your life. Maybe, like Moses, you've struggled with comparing yourself to others or wanting to be someone else. But God had incredible things in mind for your life when He created you and that hasn't changed.

As I said at the beginning of this chapter, if not dealt with, insecurities will affect every area of your life. You don't have to worry about who you are or are not, when you trust in who God is. I'll leave you with a prayer I wrote down and pray every morning to combat my insecurities. Feel free to use it for yourself.

Lord, keep me from relying on my own talents instead of what You can do through me. Keep me from trying to become like or mimic someone else. I thank you for the incredible person You have created me to be and how You're going to use me.

FIGHTING FEAR

It's fascinating what we can learn about the human condition from scientific studies. I read about a study researchers conducted with barracuda and bait fish. They put a barracuda in a tank with a bunch of bait fish. Naturally, the barracuda immediately ate the bait fish. After this happened they put more bait fish in the tank, but this time they used a pane of glass to block the barracuda from getting to them.

Out of instinct the barracuda went after the fish but smacked into the glass. A couple of minutes later, the ferocious animal would come back and try again only to run into the glass a second time. The barracuda repeated this process over and over until it finally gave up. Eventually, it got to the point where the glass was removed and the barracuda wouldn't go after the fish because it thought the glass was still there.

His environment had completely changed, but the barracuda's perception of it was the same. With the invisible barrier removed, the only thing keeping him from eating the bait fish was now the barrier that had been established in his mind.[1]

It's funny how small changes to an environment can make a big impact.

Every fall and spring the organization I work for puts on a large conference for college students and young adults. For a weekend we pack out a hotel in downtown Rochester, New York, as over seven hundred students descend on the city. As you can imagine, there is a lot of hard work that goes into setting up for an event of this size. So, we drive to the hotel the day before and begin the process of building the stage, hanging lights, and plugging in sound equipment. No matter how many times we've done this, there are normally a few hiccups along the way.

A few months ago we were setting up for our fall event and carrying large equipment cases to the elevator when, suddenly, the elevator stopped working. Thankfully, there were two elevators, but when you have a lot to unload, losing half the elevator space can really slow down the operation. We looked around the elevator that was stuck and couldn't figure out what could be keeping it from moving. After a couple of minutes, we gave up and went back to using just the one working elevator. As we continued unpacking, one of the hotel staff started investigating to see if they could determine what was keeping the elevator from moving.

A little while later, one of the guys I was working with came and announced that they had gotten the elevator working again. What had caused the downtime? Someone had dropped a plastic fork down one of the cracks. We hadn't seen the fork when looking around, but it turned out this small object was blocking this powerful elevator that can carry over a thousand pounds. It's amazing how one small plastic fork could cripple something so large.

It's amazing to me how just like the plastic fork and the pane of glass with the barracuda, one small thing that is nearly invisible can deter us from accomplishing great things. As you may have guessed from the title of this chapter, the one small thing I'm referring to is fear. At the burning bush, Moses wrestled with insecurity, but I'm sure he was facing his fears as well. God told him to go back to the land that he had fled fearing he'd be killed. As far as he knew, there was still a bounty on his head for the murder he had committed. He probably thought he could be arrested the moment he crossed back into the country.

Thankfully, God assured Moses that all who had wanted to kill him in Egypt were now dead. So, he chose to believe God and face his greatest fear. Fear is a small force that can destroy big dreams. It almost stopped Moses from delivering God's people out of decades of slavery. Overcoming fear can be the turning point in a decision and in the lives of those it impacts. Just ask the Israelites.

If we are not careful, our fears lead to worries and the process of worrying can quickly consume our lives. Jesus knew this about worrying and addressed it in His Sermon on the Mount saying, "Who of you by being worried can add a single hour to his life?" (Matthew 6:27, NASB). My wife and I have determined not to let the forces of fear and worry drive our decisions. When we have a decision to make, we've actually started to ask ourselves, "Are we making this decision out of fear?" If you start asking yourself this same question, you'll be surprised at how often fear could have affected you.

As my daughter approached school age, we agonized over where to send her for school. I had grown up going to a Christian school and my wife had attended a private Catholic school. The thought of our daughter going to a public school was difficult for both of us, but we wanted for her whatever God said was best. Our options were the local public school, which everyone raved about, a Christian school in the area which cost about as much as a nearby community college, or doing homeschool.

While my wife has experience teaching and would have done a great job with homeschool, our daughter is incredibly social and something wasn't sitting right with us about keeping her at home. We were willing to make the sacrifice of paying for the Christian school, but it would mean a very large commitment for our family that would tie up most of our finances and then some. As we thought and prayed about this important decision, we realized that all of our pastors and many families in our church were comfortable sending their children to the public school, but the fear of how that would affect our daughter still gripped us. Not only were we fearful of her being taught principles that we disagreed with, but we were also fearful of making the wrong decision.

Eventually, through prayer, God assured us that He would take care of her and protect her no matter what decision we made. We talked and realized that we had let fear frame the conversation instead of letting God guide us. In the end, we decided to send her to the public school. Just a couple of days later, we attended an informational meeting at the school for parents. As we met teachers, toured the school, and heard about the programs they offered, we were amazed at how perfect the school seemed for our daughter. Over the next week, we started to share with her about the school and all that she would get to do and her worries about going started to turn to excitement. We had changed the way we were framing the discussion and it freed us up to make the right decision.

Fear is kind of like being the last person standing on your team in a game of dodgeball. Everyone is throwing balls at you and you're desperately trying to avoid them. The chances of making a comeback are slim. But if you only dodge the balls, you'll never win. You have to start catching the balls and throwing them back to have a chance. When you feel bombarded by your fears, you can't just avoid them, you have to take them on. The acceptance of fear is assurance of a minimized life.

This past fall we were invited by friends to go pick apples and pears at their house. They had bought a house where previous owners had grown a small orchard of about fifteen fruit trees. The crop had been so plentiful this past year that they couldn't keep up with all the fruit they were getting. We took our two children along and had great fun picking the apples and pears, although I think both of our children ate much more than they picked.

My daughter was just about turning four years old and wanting more independence each day. She would climb

THE ACCEPTANCE OF FEAR IS ASSURANCE OF A MINIMIZED LIFE.

up on the ladder and want to pick the fruit, but once she got up more than a couple of steps, she became afraid of falling. I was right behind her on the ladder telling her to trust me, that I wouldn't let her fall, but she still was having trouble overcoming her fear and getting up the confidence to climb higher.

Eventually, she got to the point where she stayed up for a little time, but she still wanted me to pick the fruit. She was within reach of the fruit, but she couldn't trust me enough to reach out and grab it, even when I had my arm around her holding her, clearly preventing her from falling.

Just like my daughter couldn't take hold of the fruit because fear was holding her back, fear often keeps us from taking hold of the fruit and the blessings that God wants to give us. For example, perhaps God has spoken to you about taking a new job, but you're afraid of leaving what you know behind and worried about whether you'll make enough money to survive. Or, you know you could benefit from asking a leader to mentor you, but you're afraid of rejection.

Jesus addressed fear and worry by confronting them and challenging us to put things into perspective. He said, "Seek first His kingdom and His righteousness, and all these things will be given to you as well. Therefore do not worry about tomorrow, for tomorrow will worry about itself. Each day has enough trouble of its own" (Matthew 6:33-34, NIV). If we let ourselves get caught up in worry and fear, we'll miss out on a lot of wonderful experiences.

I once heard it said that fear is the greatest destroyer of purpose in your life. I've seen many people battle with fear, and I've witnessed the toll it takes on them. Fear can paralyze us to the point where we are unable to make decisions, enjoy the life God has given us, and sometimes it even causes us to miss out on the call God has placed on our lives.

As I said earlier, fear is a small force that can destroy big dreams. For many, though, fear is no small force. It is powerful and gripping. Moses was having a lot of trouble shaking his fear of what would happen to him if he returned to Egypt. The only way he could overcome his fear of going back was by trusting what God had told Him. God had said to him, "Certainly, I will be with you" (Exodus 3:12, NASB). It was hard for Moses to accept that, but once he chose to take God at His word, then fear was replaced with the boldness Moses needed to approach the pharaoh and stand his ground.

Moses had a choice to make. Would he stick with the simplistic life tending sheep in the desert? Or would he go to Egypt and do what God had created him for? He could either run from his fears or run at them. God had promised that he would be with him. Now he had to decide whether or not he would go where God had created him to go and do what He had created him to do. Likewise, it can be hard to face our fears, even if we know that God is with us. When you don't know what's going on, when you're discouraged, when you feel like you can't figure out what direction you're going, when you feel afraid of the future, when you have a hard choice to make, God says, "Certainly, I will be with you."

My wife and I battled with fear when it came to having children, even though we knew that God was with us. When we got married, we decided to hold off on having children. Eventually, we started to think we may never want children. Years went by and neither of us was growing any more fond of the idea. We saw how challenging it was to raise children and how much it affected the lives of our friends. We knew that if we had completely dependent, little offspring, it would affect every area of our lives and, frankly, we really liked our life the way it was. God had to tell us three times, through three different people encouraging us over the course of a year, that it was time to start having children, before we came around and decided to trust God.

Even then, when Cheryl got pregnant with our daughter, we were terrified. She was terrified of all the changes it would bring, and I was scared of raising a girl since I had grown up with all boys. Through it all we said, "Your will be done, God, not ours." And as we've put God at the center and let Him guide and direct our path, we've found His ways are better than ours and only He knows what will truly bring satisfaction in life. Parenting hasn't always been easy, but we realized that God's grace is sufficient to overcome all our fears and give us what we need to be good parents.

We let fear have its way in our lives because we see our problems as bigger than our God. The thought of having

WE LET FEAR HAVE ITS WAY IN OUR LIVES BECAUSE WE SEE OUR PROBLEMS AS BIGGER THAN OUR GOD.

children and what that would entail was so daunting to us that we elevated our comfort and selfishness above asking God what He would want us to do with our lives. When we realize how big our God is, we see how small our problems are. It turns out that Cheryl is an amazing mother and I quickly learned how to be daddy to a baby girl. Each time my wife has gotten pregnant we have still struggled, knowing that another baby will drastically change our lives and our comfort will be challenged, but God didn't call us to live comfortably.

In fact, any good thing we want in life will usually come through a process of discomfort. Think about when you decide you're going to lose weight and get healthy or when you decide to get your master's degree. The fear that we fight against comes from the unknown and the comfort that we must overthrow to achieve the dreams God has given us.

So, how do we fight fear to achieve those dreams? I mentioned earlier how Moses had to choose to run toward his fear and face it head on. Sometimes the quickest way to defeat fear is to actually face it. And then do it again and again. When I was younger, I was afraid of riding roller coasters. Eventually, I got up the nerve to ride one and, while it was a scary experience, I came away having enjoyed it.

However, for years after that, I was still scared to ride any roller coaster that went upside down. I had this irrational fear that somehow going upside down would be much worse of a thrill than the fun that I got from riding other coasters. My family would plead with me to give it a try every time we went to an amusement park, but I just sat off to the side waiting for them to get through the line.

Finally, one year when we went to Disney World, they kept pestering me so much that they finally convinced me to give it a try. There was a ride called the Rock 'n' Roller Coaster featuring Aerosmith. My family's argument was that the roller coaster was in the dark so I'd never see the upside down part coming and wouldn't have time to be afraid.

If there's one thing that's true, it's that we often fear the things we can't see more than the things we can. Instead of not being frightened, I was scared out of my mind for the entire ride. The whole thing was over within a minute, but for me that minute felt longer and more tortuous than a three hour flight with a screaming baby.

I wish I could tell you I came away loving that experience and now go on roller coasters that go upside down all the time, but, in the end, I didn't really like it. What I have found is that I'm no longer scared of going on those kinds of rides. I determined that I didn't like them, but I've ridden some since then to participate in the experience with friends. I've also tried other types of thrill rides that I never would have before, and I ended up loving those. The fear that once held me captive no longer has power over me, because I decided to run at it instead of running away from it.

It's been surprising for me to contrast my experience (fearing upside-down roller coasters until my early teens) to that of my three-year-old daughter at the amusement park. Last summer was the first time she was big enough to go on more than just the kiddie rides. We went with family and started with the small rides, then worked our way up to the bigger rides.

By the time we asked if she'd like to ride the scrambler, she was all about it. She burst out in laughter as we whizzed around at high speeds. The next thing I knew, she was asking to go on the Pirate Ship. It took me until I was like twelve years old to get the nerve up for going on the Pirate Ship. As you probably gathered, I was a little bit of a chicken growing up. But here our little three-year-old was giggling with delight while we went fifty feet up in the air and my mother-in-law sat watching from afar due to her fear of heights.

As I considered why our daughter enjoyed these rides so much, I think a big part of it was the people she was surrounded by. As the day went on, she became more and more adventurous. We were all encouraging her, and she trusted us. The people she was with helped her feel safe, and it inspired her to be fearless.

Looking back at my experiences with upside-down roller coasters and the experience of my daughter at the theme park, I can see that one of the biggest hurdles we face when overcoming fear is the one that exists within our minds. Paul noticed the same thing writing to Timothy, "For God has not given us the spirit of fear; but of power, and of love, *and of a sound mind*" (2 Timothy 1:7, KJV, emphasis mine).

We can create a fear in our minds so much so that it eventually becomes a stronghold and overtakes us. U.S. President Franklin D. Roosevelt, who was stricken with polio at the age of thirty-nine and confined to a wheelchair from the resulting paralysis, acknowledged the power of fear saying, "Men are not prisoners of fate, but only prisoners of their own minds."

Instead of rehearsing thoughts that help us feel safe and strong, we rehearse thoughts of fear that cause us to feel weak and powerless. These are the types of thoughts that Paul said we should "take captive to make them obedient to Christ" (2 Corinthians 10:5, NIV). For many of us, taking captive these thoughts means embracing a complete renewal of our minds.

When I was a young boy, my dad bought a house that needed a lot of updating. Many of the walls were made of wood paneling or plaster. I still remember the wall in our living room that displayed a scene of ducks in a swamp. It looked like it should be in the den of an eighteenth century big-game hunter with a curly mustache.

Over the years my dad worked long hours renovating this old house with me often by his side assisting. We had to tear everything out because it was so old and outdated. As we opened up more walls, we discovered more issues. The walls had been filled with spray foam insulation that most likely was filled with asbestos, and the knob and tube wiring from the early 1900's was so antiquated there was the danger that it could start a house fire. It became a much bigger project than what we originally anticipated.

We ended up replacing all the wiring and insulation in most of the house. Similarly, our minds may need more updating and renovating than we think. At one time, knob and tube wiring and spray foam insulation made sense to people, but they don't now.

At one time, you believed a way of thinking made sense, but when you realize you've let fear and thoughts of insecurity overtake you, everything must be torn out and renovated in your mind.

When my dad and I finished working on that house it looked entirely different. If you viewed it from the outside it was pretty similar, except for a coat of paint, but when you stepped inside it was almost unrecognizable. As you fight fear with God's help and confront the things that have held you back, you might find that your life looks completely different.

Just as years went by with no one updating that house until my parents moved in, over the years we form habits or patterns in our way of thinking that must be changed. We must begin to form new habits by following Paul's instructions – taking our thoughts captive one at a time and remembering that God has not given us a spirit of fear, but one of a sound mind.

Maybe you're asking yourself, "Why is he talking about things like insecurities and fear in a book about navigating life after college?" Because we must overcome these things if we are to live out the purposes God has for us. I know that God has some incredible plans and purposes for you. He declares it in His word. Some of those plans will look impossible if you only see them through a mind that has not yet been renewed.

Pastor and author Bill Johnson writes in his book *Dreaming With God*, "We'll know when our mind is truly renewed, because the impossible will look logical."[2] As you take thoughts captive and renew your mind, you might look similar on the outside, but your life will be radically changed on the inside. Instead of resigning yourself to a minimized life like Moses had tending sheep in the wilderness, you'll be able to defeat the fear that has plagued you and move forward in maximizing the life God has given you.

So, if you want to live a more satisfied life, you'll need to defy fear and all the pitfalls that come with it. You'll need to make radical decisions like removing people from your life who discourage you (if it's someone very close like a spouse, don't look to remove them, but rather try to have honest dialogue with them about the change that needs to happen) and surrounding yourself with those who will speak encouragement and inspire you. You'll need to renovate your mind with God's help and run at your fears instead of from them. When you do those things you'll be more empowered to step into the purposes God has for your life.

FINDING YOUR PURPOSE

You've probably wondered before what God's will is for your life. In fact, there's a good chance you've agonized over that question from time to time. Like many, I thought about it a lot as college graduation approached. We often have this idea that our lives have a grandiose purpose and if we don't make the right decision at the right moment then we'll miss it. We view it like a just-out-of-reach balloon that floats up into the sky never to be seen again.

You do have an incredible purpose. In fact, I believe the purpose God has designed you for is far greater than you realize. I once heard my pastor say, "To deny you have something great to offer is to actually diminish the greatness of God in you." God has something great prepared for you and you can't miss it unless you choose to ignore it. What's encouraging to me is that even when Moses committed murder, he couldn't miss his purpose. Even decades later when he struggled with insecurity and fear, he couldn't miss the calling God had for him. Moses made some huge mistakes and yet, by God's grace, he was still able to experience the purposes God had for his life.

It's funny how we get so caught up worrying that one mistake will ruin the entire course of our lives. Surely, there are consequences to our actions and so we must be vigilant to avoid sin, but God is sovereign and already knows the story of our lives from beginning to end.

We have free will, so it's up to us to make wise decisions and be good stewards of the life He's given us. But when we make bad decisions (just think of that girl or guy you dated in high school) God can lovingly put us back on track and can even use those mistakes to better shape our story and help others.

Your purpose isn't so lofty and mystical that you'll never be able to grab hold of it. And it's also not so minimal that it will be easy to attain. God has something great in store for you and to discover what it is and take hold of those things, it will take patience and determination.

Something to note about Moses' experience with the burning bush is that it wasn't just God pursuing him. We picture this bush burning up and assume that God must have done all the work, but the account in the book of Exodus tells us that God didn't speak to Moses from the bush until Moses chose to go over to the bush.

Now, surely a flaming bush that wasn't burning up was an intriguing sight and would have caught the attention of most, but the point is that Moses had to engage in the process with God. Finding our unique purpose is a wonderful journey that involves us pursuing God and Him revealing Himself to us.

I use the word journey because fully discovering who you are and what you're meant to do with your life usually takes time. In our fast-paced, give-it-to-me-now world, we don't like hearing that. But there's great joy and enrichment that can come from the journey if you embrace it instead of being frustrated by it. Remember that God tells us in the Bible not to "despise small beginnings" (Zechariah 4:10, NLT). Most people who have incredible accomplishments took time to get there.

Take legendary coach John Wooden for example. Wooden was a player who eventually went on to coach the UCLA men's basketball team. Under his leadership, the team won ten championships in twelve years. During one stretch, his teams won a record setting 88 consecutive games!

But what many don't realize is that he coached the Bruins for fifteen years before he won his first championship. It took over a decade of investment and honing his craft before he was able to see results. In today's world many universities would have fired him before he had the chance to build a great program because they want to see fast results.

The first key to finding your purpose is that it comes through self-discovery. Think of self-discovery like an intricate origami design. Origami is the art of folding paper into various designs. You might remember origami as those little paper birds the smart kids in your class would make when you were in middle school.

If you want to understand how the piece of origami was made, you'll need to unfold it, paying close attention to every detail. It's amazing how detailed origami can be. One piece, the Red Sea Urchin designed by Hans Birkeland, has 913 folds that require over 2,700 creases to be manipulated. God has created us to be even more intricate than origami, and so you must be aware that unfolding and determining who you are will take time.

In preparation for this book, I interviewed a number of leaders at different stages in life to ask them what they've learned about finding their purpose and being successful. Across the board the theme that came up over and over is that a person's purpose is a lot less about "the what" and much more about "the who." If you want to know what you're supposed to do in life, you'll need to discover who God created you to be.

I've found this principle to be true in my own life, and it's my belief that something similar happened with Moses. Remember, Moses caught a glimpse of his purpose when he stopped the Egyptian from beating an Israelite. He just went about it the wrong way and at the wrong time. But that interaction shows us that God had put a burden and desire in Moses' heart to save His people.

I'm sure when Moses fled to the wilderness, there was a lot of time for him to figure out who he was in the years that followed. Moses probably did some serious soul searching during that time. Trials and disappointments are often the fire that teach us more about ourselves and what's most important. When I went through that challenging time of not getting the job promotion I was expecting, God used that to show me more about who I am. When that happened, I asked the Lord multiple times what I should be doing with my life and questioned if I had heard Him wrong about the purposes and calling He has for me.

As I looked inward and asked God to show me more about myself and who He's created me to be, I began to see things I had never seen before. I learned more about the gifts He had given me and realized that I didn't have gifts and talents in other areas that I had been pouring myself into. Essentially, I became more aware of my strengths and weaknesses. Some of this awareness came through prayer and other times it came through the coaching and mentoring I was receiving from leaders I respected.

Finding your purpose starts with asking some questions and the first is, "Who am I?" When we begin to pay attention to the way we tick, the things that stir our hearts and that excite us, we can start taking steps to develop those areas. I went through this process several years ago, but my experience echoes what one of the leaders I interviewed told me about discovering your purpose.

Steve Shadrach, a friend who has worked with college students and young adults for many years, said to me, "I sought to 'grow into business' rather than 'go into business.' In other words, don't tell young people to pick a career or discern a mysterious calling, just start radically and practically and regularly obeying the commands of Scripture to pray, study the Word, witness, disciple, reach the world for Christ. In the process of applying themselves to their personal growth and ministry, and in community with other 'obeyers,' they will start to discover their passions, gifts, strengths, weaknesses, and ultimately find their vision and calling. It is a process though, not an event or decision."

Like Steve pointed out, you can't just wait for something to magically appear to you. You will discover your purpose as you faithfully pour into the place that God has planted you in this season, whether that's as a doctor seeing patients, a student studying to get through grad school, or as a cashier at the local Wal-Mart.

Maybe you're still not sure how to start this process. This is where self-awareness is important and the way you get better in this area is by consciously paying attention to yourself on a daily basis and asking honest friends for input.

As you go through your day, what are you thinking in a given moment and why are you thinking it? What kinds of tasks and hobbies leave you feeling refreshed and inspired and which ones leave you feeling exhausted and depleted? If you had unlimited time and resources, what would you choose to do? What do people praise you for or point out as your strengths?

There are many different ways to learn about who God made you to be. Take some personality tests online to learn more about yourself. You'll be surprised at how accurate they can be and what they teach you about yourself. Notice what causes or people groups you have a burden for. Think about what needs around you stir your heart so much that you feel you must get involved.

Another friend of mine named Bob who helps lead a missions organization calls these our core values. He says, "More important, for me, is to build core values in one's life. These will guide our decisions, regardless of where ministry or work will take us. Do you always want to work with people? Serve disadvantaged people? Work to reach unsaved people overseas? You can build values into your life that reflect these desires, and you can fulfill them in different forms, depending on what your current line of work allows."

We can get so caught up wasting time on our phones and running from thing to thing that we neglect paying attention to the clues God has already placed within us as to how He wants to use us. You might need to take some time to sit and reflect at the end of the day. Consider the questions I gave you, then write down your thoughts and observations. After you do this for a couple of weeks, you'll begin to see a pattern.

Just remember that there's a difference between things you enjoy and things you are passionate about. For instance, my wife has an imaginary blog. That sounds strange, so let me explain. She is hilarious and sees the world from a perspective that many don't. At times I envy her wit and quick humor. People find her so funny that when we see them in public they regularly comment on her Facebook posts about our kids and many tell her she should write a book or a blog.

She's considered writing a blog at multiple points, but what we've decided is that she would write an amazing blog for about a month. That would be the extent of it and her massive readership (because she's so great) would end up disappointed and wanting more. It would be like when J.K. Rowling ended the *Harry Potter* series. Ok, maybe I'm overdoing it a little. The point is, while she's incredibly funny and a good writer, we both know she's not passionate enough about the idea of writing a blog to commit herself to it long term, at least not at this time in our lives. It's something she enjoys, but it's not something she's truly passionate about right now.

To find something you're passionate about, you have to think about the motivations behind it. The motivation for my wife writing a blog is that it could be fun. There's nothing wrong with fun, but fun in itself usually isn't a good enough motivation to fully commit yourself to something. Think about if you ever played a sport when you were younger. I loved playing sports, but most of the time it was something I enjoyed more than something I was passionate about.

I had fun scoring a goal in soccer, winning a basketball game, or traveling with the football team during my high school years. I didn't even mind going to practice most of the time. But if push came to shove, I wasn't going to get up at 5 a.m. to go lift and two-a-days were the bane of my existence. I just wasn't passionate enough about playing sports to make it a lifelong pursuit. This goes back to when I talked about setting goals and determining your *why*.

To make the distinction between something you enjoy and what you're truly passionate about, you need to think about what you could see yourself doing every day.

Playing sports was, and still is, fun for me, but it wasn't something that fueled me on a daily basis. Even if you're someone who is passionate enough about playing sports to put the time and commitment in, there's another factor to take into account. Do you have the necessary talent to be great at it or can you learn those skills? Discovering your strengths and weaknesses will point your compass in the right direction, but just as seasons come and go, how you apply your strengths and gifts usually takes several forms throughout your life.

My friend Bob touched on this in my interview with him saying, "I don't think there's necessarily a single purpose that will define our lives, if by purpose we're referring to a life and ministry calling. Most of the respected leaders in my life have had many different seasons define their work life: pastor, author, international speaker, director of a non-profit, college president. And that's just one guy! Our productive, working years last a long time, and I think the focused person who will pursue one purpose in life is rare."

I agree with Bob and that's why it's so important to know yourself. When situations arise or opportunities present themselves, you'll have more clarity on whether it's something you should say yes to or something you should avoid. This is especially true when we're talking about opportunities that are very appealing, but aren't the right fit for the way you're designed. Over the last few years I've been intentionally seeking to understand myself better and how God has wired me. I've been paying attention to the ways I think and why I think that way.

Author and theologian Frederick Buechner reflecting on vocation wrote, "The place where God calls you to is the place where your deep gladness and the world's deep hunger meet."[1] We typically think of our vocation as our job, but the Latin root of the word vocation means "calling." A calling has much deeper meaning than just being a job. You'll likely hold many jobs as time goes on, but your calling is something that provides the framework for where you'll succeed and what you'll find the most satisfaction in. It's through being diligent, learning about how God has made you, and developing your skills, that you'll eventually reach your calling. In other words, we can find the calling God has for us by first looking at the *who* and then the *what*. You must marry who God has made you to be with the skills He has given you.

One morning while taking a shower I was not thinking about much of anything when I suddenly heard God speaking to me about my purpose. But He wasn't giving me clearly outlined action steps. It was more like overarching words that spoke to the ways I most enjoy serving others. The three words I heard Him say were communicating, connecting and creating. I wrote these three words down and then under each one wrote another word that described what these would look like when carried out. Under communicating I wrote inspiring, under connecting, empowering, and under creating, pioneering.

I share these with you to explain that these three words – communicating, connecting, creating – are words I can review every time I decide whether or not to take up an opportunity that presents itself. Knowing these I can now ask myself, "Does this enable me to communicate, connect, or create?" This is the calling God has given me that lays the framework for everything else. You can also see how these can translate to a number of different roles, careers, and projects that I might commit myself to over time. But it's not enough to know who you are and be passionate about something. You then have to develop skills in that area.

The next question to ask oneself is, "What has God given me and how can I grow in it?" When God called Moses to go into Egypt and Moses kept questioning God He asked him, "What is that in your hand?" (Exodus 4:2, ESV). God then showed Moses how he could use the staff he had been carrying as a tool for herding sheep as a means for working miracles before Pharaoh. God has given you competence in areas that align with your calling. Sometimes we overlook them because what we have seems insignificant right now. The staff Moses was carrying didn't look like much, but God can turn seemingly insignificant gifts into significant ones. Often we see these skills as insignificant because they need further development if we are to achieve the full potential God has for us.

When I first started working with college students seven years ago, one of the tasks I was given was to prepare sermons. I spoke weekly at groups we were running on campus and when traveling to visit other ministries around New York. It was apparent when I first started preaching that I had an ability to speak. I was well-spoken and the messages I shared impacted people. This was confirmed by people who encouraged me and told me that sermons I shared blessed them. But I knew that my communication skills could be better.

Over the years I've taken classes, read books, listened to other preachers, and preached as often as given the opportunity so that I could further improve upon the natural gifting God has given me in this area. I know I still have so many ways I can keep getting better, so I'm not content to think I've arrived. I've identified what God has given me, but I'm still regularly asking, "How can I grow in it?" With the power of the Internet, it's amazing how easy it is to grow in practically any skill for free or little cost.

It's also surprising how many people want to help you grow if you're willing to put yourself out there. This doesn't always come easy. When I first decided that I was going to ask to meet with some leaders I knew, I was hesitant. The kind of people I wanted to learn from were busy and I just couldn't imagine them wanting to take time out of their schedules to help me.

What I found was exactly the opposite. Most successful people have gotten to where they are by serving others. So, when I approached them they were happy to offer their time to teach me valuable principles they had learned.

I guarantee you there are people in your life – pastors, teachers, your parent's friends, business people – who would happily give you some of their time if you asked. I've met with leaders in my area to learn about a whole host of subjects from preaching to being a better husband to how to raise children. If you're willing to be a little vulnerable and open yourself up to constructive feedback, you'll see explosive growth in your life.

Make it a goal to connect with someone you want to learn from this week. Look for people who have traits that you admire and want to see in yourself. Ask them if you could meet with them to learn and grow in those areas. Let them dictate the time and length of your meeting. Then come prepared with questions that will help facilitate the conversation.

You'll be surprised at how much you can learn from somebody over breakfast or lunch, and they may even offer to meet with you again. I've found that one of the most missing aspects for someone in their twenties is a mentor, but many people are excited to serve in this way if given the opportunity.

So you've started asking the questions, "Who am I?" and "What has God given me and how can I grow in it?" The third vital question to the process of finding your purpose is, "What do I want to be known for?" This is the kind of question that makes you think about what you want people to say about you at your funeral. Another way to put this question is, "What kind of legacy do I want to leave?"

This third question will help you really clarify what's most important. Take the story of a Swedish businessman named Alfred, for example. Toward the end of the nineteenth century, Alfred sat down to breakfast.

As he sipped his coffee, he began to look through the morning newspaper. He was quite shocked to see that he was on the front page. Of course, he was surprised, but he was even more surprised to realize that it was his obituary.

The newspaper had confused him with his brother, Ludvig, who died in the East Indies. As Alfred read the article, his surprise turned to dismay. He read phrases like "Merchant of Munitions," "Dealer of Destruction," and "Peddler of Death." Alfred was known for such deadly inventions as dynamite and ballistic.

Seeing his name combined with those terrible phrases, he made a decision. He got in his carriage, traveled to an office, and wrote a brand new will. He asked that the rest of his estate be invested into a fund, "the interest on which shall be annually distributed in the form of prizes to those who, during the preceding year, shall have conferred the greatest benefit to mankind."[2]

This document established the Nobel Peace Foundation. Today, the Nobel Peace Foundation gives out the Nobel Peace Prize, widely regarded as the most prestigious award available in the fields of literature, medicine, physics, chemistry, peace and economics. And this world-renowned award came about all because Alfred Nobel asked, "What do I want to be known for?"

What I like most about this question is that it encourages me to dream big. You may feel as if you're not in a place to accomplish great things now, but if you look at your life with the end in mind, it's easier to see yourself achieving significant dreams because you have decades to work at it. This is the activation part of the process because when you answer this question you can then begin living intentionally to accomplish the dreams God has given you.

Don't shortchange yourself on this question. President Woodrow Wilson said, "You are not here merely to make a living. You are here in order to enable the world to live more amply, with greater vision, with a finer spirit of hope and achievement. You are here to enrich the world, and you impoverish yourself if you forget the errand."

Whether you realize it or not, we serve an incredible God who has incredible plans for your life. It's important to remember that your purpose is completely wrapped up in God's great purpose. Paul says in the Bible, "We know that in all things God works for the good of those who love him, who have been called according to His purpose" (Romans 8:28, NIV).

Your calling is based on His purpose, His plans for your life, for those around you, and for the entire world. He's been writing a great story since the beginning of time and now He's given you a chance to be part of that amazing story. The famous evangelist C.T. Studd said it this way in a now famous poem, "Only one life, 'twill soon be past; only what's done for Christ will last."

So, whatever you find yourself doing, it should be centered around the work of advancing His Kingdom. When Jesus taught the disciples how to pray He used the words, "Your Kingdom come, Your will be done" (Matthew 6:10, ESV).

That should be our prayer in everything we do. When we center our lives around seeing God's Kingdom come and His will being done, then we know the things we pursue will have a lasting impact. Your purpose isn't meant to just affect the present or even the next few decades; it's meant to alter eternity. I don't say that to make you nervous or to pressure you, but rather to motivate you that no matter what you put your hands to, it can have eternal significance.

You may think that you don't look like much or have much to offer, but look at what God did in the life of Moses. He was born into slavery with a decree to be put to death. His mother placed him in a basket floating on the Nile River in faith that God would protect him. Not only did he never work as a slave, he grew up in the palace of the most powerful kingdom at that time.

Even when he committed murder and fled to the wilderness for decades, God had a powerful plan for his life and used him to redeem an entire nation. If God can use a cowardly murderer who should have been killed before his first birthday to free an entire nation from the grip of slavery, He can surely use you.

You may not know your purpose, but just like Moses, God has written your story even before birth and He has an awesome plan for you. You have a God-given purpose. If you don't believe me, then ask yourself why God would spend so much time carefully crafting someone who had no purpose. He has a plan for every person and every thing He creates. And something powerful happens when who you are merges with what God wants to do in the earth. But even if you understand that God has great plans for you, the concept of learning the legacy God wants you to leave still might be daunting.

Honestly, this question is the hardest one for me to answer. I have a general answer to this, but I've struggled at times to understand something more specific. Sometimes trying to think about where I want to be forty years from now can be overwhelming given that the last ten years of my life have gone nothing like what I expected. How could I possibly pretend to know where God wants to take me? In fact, I believe that God wants to do such great things in my life that I wouldn't be able to fully understand or even envision them if I tried right now.

Here's what I do know. Some action is better than no action. Any idea is better than no idea. Just because I don't have a full picture of what God wants to do in my life doesn't excuse me from taking any action now. I do have those three words – communicate, create, and connect – that, while they are fairly broad descriptions of what I'm called to, do provide a place to start. I can use what God has spoken to me to lean into and start taking steps on the road He has called me to, knowing that He'll show me more of the picture as I go, and the same is true for you.

So, I want to encourage you that you don't have to know all the ins and outs of what God has for you right now. We erroneously think we're supposed to have this all figured out when we enter college, but often we don't know ourselves well enough at the age of eighteen to determine where we should place our focus. It took me years to realize that those three areas are ones that I am passionate about and have defined skills in.

Remember, Moses was eighty years old before God called him to stand before Pharaoh. Hopefully you'll have a good idea of how God wants to use you before you reach eighty, but to think that you have to know exactly what you're supposed to do with your life when you're twenty-two and just out of college is absurd.

My friend Steve, who I mentioned earlier, acknowledged this process in what he shared saying, "They will spend years and years focused on their vision and calling, continuing to refine and tweak and experiment, saying yes to certain things and no to others, until at some point in life they will wake up one day and possess a definite feeling of "convergence," that sweet spot where they are doing exactly what they were made for. It is a fulfilling experience, but for this generation, who demand instant gratification, not many will pay the price, and have the patience, to stay on that road over 5-10-20+ years."

So, the question I would pose to you is, "Are you willing to pay the price? Are you willing to be patient as you figure out what God has for you?" You don't have to have all the answers now. You will never have all the answers. Discovering your purpose is a process that you can embrace and enjoy instead of being frustrated and anxious about.

It just starts with asking the three questions: "Who am I?", "What has God given me and how can I grow in it?", and "What do I want to be known for?" Once you've begun to answer those, then you can start to take action.

LIVING OUT YOUR PURPOSE

Just knowing your purpose isn't enough. You must put boots on the ground to actually accomplish God's purpose for your life. It's like anything else we do in life. The other night my family finished eating dinner and I got up to start loading the dishwasher. As I was putting cups and plates away, my two-year-old son began bringing me dishes from the table and, with my help, putting them in the dishwasher. In a moment of inspiration I thought to myself, this is why I had kids!

My wife pointed out that he was only doing this because he had seen the example I set. Now, I could think about clearing the table. I could even talk about clearing the table. But that in itself wouldn't motivate my children to do it. I have to actually do the work of loading the dirty dishes for the table to get cleaned up.

In the same way, living out your purpose requires faith coupled with action. You can't have one without the other. In fact, the Bible speaks to this. The author of the book of Hebrews said that without faith it is impossible to please God. But then in the next book, James, the brother of Jesus, told us that faith without works is dead. I can have all the faith in the world that someone will be healed, and God may heal them without me. But, to be a part of that healing event, I have to put action to my faith and go pray for that person. Similarly, I can go pray for that person to be healed, but if I don't trust God will do it in the first place, it's unlikely I will be a part of someone's healing encounter.

Moses must have been filled with faith after speaking to the God of the universe through a burning bush that wasn't being consumed. Don't you wish that God would show up with a booming voice speaking through your TV and make your purpose as obvious as He did with Moses? It might creep you out at first, but talk about easy. Even though Moses fought against what God was telling him because he felt unqualified, he must have finally received some level of confidence as God continued to tell him this was the purpose He had called Moses to. But Moses had to take action or else Israel would never be freed from slavery. He had to go to Egypt and confront Pharaoh. He had to respond to what God told him and use his staff to execute the ten plagues. His actions showed that he trusted God and was willing to obey the call on his life.

There are five ways we see Moses living out his purpose. The first is that Moses had chosen to live a surrendered life before God. He decided that if God gave him this mission, he was going to do whatever God told him to. My wife and I have had some moments like that in our lives. The summer that we raised funds to go into ministry was one of those challenging seasons. We were seeing progress toward our God-given mission, but not nearly as quickly as we would have liked.

We had set a goal to be fully funded by August 15th so we could move to our new home and start working on the nearby college campuses. In the months leading up to that day, we were working like crazy to raise the money. I had quit my job halfway through the process to give fundraising my full attention. During the day, my wife and I would make phone calls for hours to set up appointments where we could share our vision and ask people to join our team. In the evenings, we went from one meeting to the next as we worked toward our goal. Often we had dinner and dessert with one couple, then rushed to the next two meetings where we were offered dessert twice more. At times I've thought that there was no such thing as too much dessert, but these occasions taught me I was wrong.

It was tiring, but we knew it was what God had called us to and nothing would deter us. We came to the week before August 15th and looked at how much we had raised. We still had only reached twenty-five percent of our monthly goal. We looked over our budget as we considered whether we should change our moving date. Some of the people we met with had given us large start-up gifts that would help sustain us for a number of months until we could raise more finances. As we went to the Lord in prayer, we kept hearing that August 15th was the date we should go. So, with trepidation and excitement we packed up our things and surrendered to what God was saying. It was scary to make that decision, but we couldn't deny what God was saying and we knew that God gave us this mission, so we were going to do whatever He told us to.

When I was young, my parents modeled for me the practice of asking God first before making any decision. I'm so grateful they showed me the power of living a surrendered life. I've seen over the years that a surrendered life is a rewarding life. Moses chose to trust God and go to Egypt. It wasn't what he wanted to do, but he chose to do what God was telling him. We had to trust God as we stepped out in faith. When it comes down to it, I'm not willing to live a me-centered life. I know my life will be much more fulfilled if I live it with a God-centered approach.

Living out your purpose will require audacious faith as you choose to live a surrendered life before God, but it's completely worth it. That's the difference between someone who merely commits to a project and someone who has truly found their purpose. When you grab hold of your purpose, you will not hesitate to restructure your life for attaining what God has called you to. It doesn't have to take place all at once like it did with Moses. It may unfold in steps over time, but there will be a significant shift that happens in your life as you place your trust in God.

Once Moses chose to live a surrendered life, the second thing he did was take risks. Going back to Egypt was the first risk, as I've already covered. Then standing before Pharaoh demanding freedom for the Israelites required a whole new set of risks that concluded with leading millions of people out of Egypt. If you are to live out your particular purpose, it will require some sort of risk. Albert Einstein once said, "A ship is always safe at shore, but that is not what it was built for."

My wife and I took a big risk when we moved to another city having only raised twenty-five percent of our necessary funds. A couple of weeks after we moved, our new boss called us into his office to talk over our finances. We explained our progress and our aspirations of raising more money quickly. He was rightfully concerned and asked if we would consider one of us taking up a part-time job to supplement our income. We in turn asked him for a day to spend time together praying and seeking what God would have us do. As we spent time in prayer with worship music playing, a song came on that struck a chord in our hearts. It was a song by the band Jars of Clay, and the chorus repeated the line, "If I had two hands doing the same thing. Lifted high, lifted high." We knew in that moment, beyond a shadow of a doubt, that we were both supposed to give our full attention to the ministry.

Now don't hear me wrong. Circumstances like this aren't a one-size-fits-all kind of deal. I'm sharing our story as an example, not a blueprint. I've seen others who have been faced with similar situations and eventually they had to take on a part-time job. There is nothing wrong with that. We took a risk, knowing that we had heard from

God, and it paid off as God showed Himself faithful in our finances time and time again.

We met with our boss the next day and shared with him what we felt God had spoken to us in prayer. He was surprised by our answer, knowing we had chosen a much more difficult and uncertain path, but he was supportive. I think deep down he admired our bold, all-in attitude.

The risks you have to take may look similar. You might be facing a challenging financial decision – like deciding to take on three extra jobs so you can pay your student loans off faster. Or you may decide to take a job that pays less, but you know will bring you more satisfaction.

Maybe the risks you'll have to take will look different, like breaking up with a boyfriend or girlfriend who you know is holding you back, or going back to school for eight years to get your PhD, or realizing that living in your parents' basement comes with an expiration date and it's time to get your own place. Whatever the risks are that you face, you'll have to overcome the fear of failure to face them with confidence. But be encouraged because, even if you do fail at times, you'll fit right in with the rest of us.

Famous author and leadership guru John Maxwell says, "God uses people who fail – 'cause there aren't any other kind around."[1] I faced failure when I chose to put myself out there and apply for the position of executive director and was turned down. I didn't let that disappointment keep me from moving forward as I continued to serve God where He had placed me. You choose whether failures become dead ends or simply speed bumps in your journey.

I'm sure Moses felt like he was a failure each time he executed a plague and Pharaoh still refused to let the people go. When you confront failure, you must face it the way Moses did – by being persistent – which is the third ingredient for living out your purpose. Moses probably got discouraged as the plagues continued and Pharaoh's heart got harder, but he continued to do what God had called him to. As you live out your purpose there will be times when you get discouraged, times that you question if this really is God's will for your life, and possibly even times when others try to stop you from accomplishing what God has called you to.

Just remember that if you're doing what God has called you to, then you need to be persistent. Persistence in trying times was what defined the career of many notable figures in the Bible. Isaiah was sent by God to a people who wouldn't listen to him. I can't imagine continuing to speak to a people who wouldn't listen to me, but Isaiah is quoted many times in the Gospels as Jesus fulfills his prophecies. His persistence in speaking the words God gave him would confirm that Jesus was the promised Savior hundreds of years later.

John the Baptist prepared the way for Jesus by baptizing all who came to him and even was given the honor of baptizing Jesus himself. His perseverance to proclaim the truth, even when what he said wasn't popular, eventually led to his beheading.

There will be those who don't like what you have to say or try to discourage you, but stay focused on the

PERSISTENCE IN TRYING TIMES WAS WHAT DEFINED THE CAREER OF MANY NOTABLE FIGURES IN THE BIBLE.

purpose. If you have to bring it before the Lord again and ask if you're doing the right thing that is fine, but once you have regained confidence that you're in God's will, stay focused. Moses' job was not to free the Israelites in his own strength, but rather to listen to God and obey his directions. God was the one who hardened Pharaoh's heart, and He was the one who performed the miracles that would eventually free His people. Being persistent means being faithful to carry out the directions God has given you even if it seems as if everything is against you.

When you live a surrendered life, take risks, and choose to be persistent, it will require trusting God in incredible ways. Remember when Moses finally was able to lead the people out of Egypt, only to find he had led them into a trap that placed them between the Red Sea and the Egyptian army bearing down on them? The Israelites were panicked and overcome with fear as they saw the chariots racing toward them. Pharaoh had changed his mind once again and decided he really couldn't let the Israelites leave. Pharaoh's firstborn son was dead, the land lay in ruin from the plagues, and yet he was still determined to win this battle with God.

With their backs against the Red Sea, Moses had to trust God to provide a way out. The people had major trust issues. God had brought them out of Egypt in a supernatural way, but they still had trouble trusting that He knew what was best for them. They began to complain to Moses and even asserted that they would have been better off staying in Egypt. They didn't trust God, even while He was making a way for them just as He had before. Even though the people were having trouble trusting God, Moses stood firm. He said, "The Lord will fight for you; you need only to be still" (Exodus 14:14, NIV). It's pretty amazing to contemplate the trust Moses must have had in God to say that as millions of people were grumbling at him and death seemed imminent.

When you trust God like your life depends on it, He'll never let you down. In fact, He wants to bring you to the point of full dependence on Him so you know that everything you accomplish is only by His grace. There's a classic Christian saying that goes, "If God brings you to it, He'll bring you through it." This is most certainly what Moses and the Israelites were experiencing as the Red Sea parted and the waves stacked up like giant walls on either side so that they could cross on dry ground.

Moses trusted God in the face of extreme adversity and God rewarded that trust and provided for the Israelites in a miraculous way. If Moses had still been questioning whether he was doing the will of God in leading these people out of Egypt, there was certainly no question now. It's not every day that you receive confirmation of your calling by witnessing a massive sea opening up for miles so you can lead a sea of people across on dry ground. As you trust God with the calling He has placed on your life, you will see rewards from it as well.

Sure, you probably won't see Lake Ontario spreading apart so you can march thousands of people from Niagara Falls into Toronto. The confirmation of your calling will look different than that of Moses, and your calling will look much different than Moses', too. Your unique calling will require unique methods, risks, and persistence. And it will come with unique results. That's the beauty of how God has written the story of Earth. He has placed billions of people on this planet and given us each an exclusive purpose that collectively aligns with His singular purpose to save humanity.

We are privileged to be a part of this great story. That is why it's of vital importance that we take our calling seriously. Jesus was laser-focused on the purpose God had given Him. At one point when He was talking with the disciples He said, "My food is to do the will of Him who sent Me and to accomplish His work" (John 4:34, ESV). Think about the words Jesus chose for a minute. People don't usually compare doing God's will to food. So, what is Jesus getting at here? I think He's saying that if He doesn't do the will of the Father, He will literally die because doing God's will is His food. It's what He lives on.

What has been your food? Do you starve if you're not doing God's will? Are you actively living every day with your vision set squarely on living out your purpose? That's not an easy goal to set and keep, especially when there are so many things to take our time and priorities. I remember when I was in college thinking I was so busy when, really, I had all the time in the world.

I was a broadcasting major and my classes didn't require a lot of reading or papers. In my first semester my best friend and I, who was also my roommate, became friends with Steve, a guy on our hall. Steve was funny, and a little goofy, tall and skinny. He lived on Long Island and liked punk rock. The only thing we really had in common was our love for video games. We started hanging out a lot and spent hours working to defeat the latest boss or set a new record for most goals scored in a hockey tournament. With the dining hall food, we were starting to put on the pounds, but at least our thumbs were in good shape.

As Steve learned more about my broadcasting major and involvement in television production, he had an idea. He convinced my best friend and me to create a show for the campus TV station based on a hit show on MTV that involved people doing stupid things and hurting themselves. I had never in my life imagined I would be a part of a show like this. I can't even remember how he convinced us it was a good idea, but somehow he did. So, we set to work creating the show we would eventually call Campus Chaos.

We decided to do fun stunts that might be painful, but would hopefully keep us out of the hospital. We put pads on one of our friends and smashed racquetballs at him. We connected wagons by rope to cars and got pulled behind them through the street. We had Steve stand shirtless on the side of the road and successively hit him in the back with a fly swatter at increasing speeds. When we got up to 60 miles an hour it left the imprint of a crosshatch pattern that remained for over a week.

We were taking stupid to a new level and people loved it. Sometimes we were approached by "fans" in the dining hall who would say, "Hey, you're the guys from Campus Chaos!" It's amazing what you can get famous for. Well, at least a little famous.

The most memorable stunt we did came on a windy day. The college I attended was right on the shores of Lake Ontario. Because of this it would get incredibly windy and there was a day where the gusts were getting up to 90 miles per hour. I decided to strap on my rollerblades, pull out my bedsheets and ride around the campus using the sheets as a sail.

Just when I got going so fast that the thought of trying to stop was frightening, a crosswind would catch my billowing bed sheet sail, throwing me to the ground as I desperately tried to land on the grass instead of the concrete. More often than not, I landed on the concrete sidewalk, and when we were done filming I had my fair share of scratches and bruises. My sheets even had little holes in them from where I had landed. I bet you'd be surprised right about now to hear that I was a Dean's List student throughout college. It's okay if you've lost any respect for me that you might have accrued over the first seven chapters of this book. I was young and stupid.

The point is, while I look back on that show with fond memories and I have some ridiculous stories to share, it was taking time from my purpose. Thankfully, God's purpose for my life was never for me to act like an idiot and capture it all on camera. There's nothing wrong with having a little fun, but Campus Chaos had started taking all our time. Between coming up with ideas, filming everything and then spending a lot of time editing, sometimes we were spending up to 20 hours a week working on the show. It was almost like having a part-time job without the pay. And so, we decided to hang it up after just one semester.

We were all a little bummed because the project had been really fun, but when we stopped working on the show, I was able to commit more time to what God had called me to. I needed to make drawing closer to God and chasing after His plans for my life my "food." I started getting more involved in the Christian club I had joined and building relationships with people in my dorm. That club would end up playing a significant role in my college years and was the main catalyst for when God called us to work in college ministry years later. I'm still friends with many of those people I built relationships with and some of them are doing incredible work around the world.

Once you know your purpose, you need to give your best time to it. In other words, you need to make it a priority. This is the fifth element for living out your purpose. What is something you could do tomorrow to begin living with purpose? Are you actively living every day with a purpose, to accomplish something for His kingdom? There are so many simple ways you can start taking action. You don't have to have it all figured out and getting started doesn't have to be an elaborate undertaking. There's an old Chinese proverb that conveys this thought, "Every journey begins with the first step."

Start small by setting out to accomplish a goal or take steps toward a goal. You can look for opportunities to share your faith with a friend or pray for a coworker. Some days living out my purpose looks as simple as finding ways to bless my wife by doing the dishes or picking up after the kids.

There are so many ways to do this and it can be much simpler than we make it. Remember what my friend Steve said about practically and regularly looking to obey the clear commands we've been given in the Scriptures and allowing God to lovingly guide you every step of the way.

Taking these steps to live out your purpose – living a surrendered life, taking risks, being persistent, trusting God, and setting priorities – is what will bring true satisfaction and joy in life. It won't come in finding the right spouse or the right career. It won't come by working as hard and long as possible to make all the money you can. It won't even come if you surround yourself with the best of friends. God has given us this life so that we can glorify Him, and He wants us to fully enjoy it. Jesus said, "I came that they may have life and have it abundantly" (John 10:10, ESV).

God's desire is for us to truly enjoy our lives and lead others to a place where they can do the same, because when we are fulfilled in our lives and in our relationship with God, we bring Him great glory.

That's what Jesus modeled for us during His time on earth. No one was closer to the Father than Jesus. He had an incredible relationship with God. It was out of that relationship with God and knowing His purpose that He blessed all those around Him. And as they were blessed, healed, loved, and encouraged, their lives were more fulfilled and they drew closer to God.

God has invited you to be a part of that story – the story of saving mankind by calling them to the Father. It will require great risk and determination. It will require saying no to some pursuits so we can say yes to more vital ones. You will need to live a completely surrendered life. It will be challenging and draining at times, but it will also be the greatest way you could ever spend your life. It will be more abundant and fulfilling than you ever could have dreamed possible. Don't settle for anything less.

GET DIRTY, DREAM BIG

Moses led the Israelites out of Egypt, miraculously escaped through the Red Sea, and now they found themselves in the desert without food or water. God had shown Himself faithful and provided for them in amazing ways. When they escaped from Pharaoh and saw the Egyptian army swallowed by the Red Sea, their hearts leaped for joy and they praised God for all He had done. But after three days passed they were losing sight of all that. They began to complain and grumble about their situation. The people even went so far as to say that they would have been better off staying in slavery in Egypt.

They had already forgotten about the plagues God had rained down on the nation that had opposed them. They had already dismissed the sores on their backs from the whippings they had endured as slaves. They had already moved on from the joy their hearts had known as the waves of the Red Sea crashed down behind them.

Our short-term memory is often a louder voice than God's long-term faithfulness.

OUR SHORT-TERM MEMORY IS OFTEN A LOUDER VOICE THAN GOD'S LONG-TERM FAITHFULNESS.

Now, I can't fault the Israelites. I get just as angry and miserable when I'm hungry. I'm like a grizzly bear foraging through a campground while my wife and kids cower quietly in their tents. And I've never gone three whole days without food or water. The Israelites needed food to survive, but they were losing sight of the promise God had given Moses that He would take care of them and bring them into an incredibly bountiful land. Don't get so caught up in what's screaming for your attention in the present that you stop looking forward to the future God has called you to. Also, don't get so caught up in dreaming of what the future holds that you can't see the importance of being diligent in the here and now.

There's a tension we're called to live in. The tension exists between knowing we must dig in and get dirty while having a servant mindset, while also knowing we are to dream big as co-heirs with Christ who are not called to settle for less than God's best in our lives. As you determine to live out your purpose, you may find that it will take a while to get there. You may find that you have to work in a job that doesn't line up with that purpose until much later in life.

I often think that people are either the type to get dirty or dream big. I guess in my mind you are either someone who deals with details and digs into specifics, or you are someone who dreams big and whose head is always in the clouds, but that doesn't make sense. God has given you tasks to do now that pertain to your dreams and He will give you tasks to do later that pertain to your dreams. If your dreams are really big, then you can expect them to take time.

There's nothing wrong with working your way up in life. That could be called being diligent. There is something wrong with settling for less than God's best. Whether it's in choosing a spouse who has major character flaws, spending your money frivolously instead of saving it, or keeping friendships with people who are discouraging you instead of helping you grow, you can choose less than God's best. That's called being foolish.

The Israelites had to first go through the desert to get to the abundant and wonderful land God had promised them. It was a long journey before they would get there, but they couldn't settle for less than what God had for them by staying in Egypt. God had spoken to Moses about the Promised Land, so he knew the end goal. But to get there, he would need to get his "hands dirty." He would contend with plenty of challenges along the way.

You will face challenges as well. Many times those challenges will come in the form of discouragement, frustration, and self-doubt. You'll need to continue to dream big while getting "dirty." You see, there's a big difference between finding an entry-level job and being willing to work your way up versus doing something just for the money or because it seems more sensible. It's the difference between playing it long and playing it safe. With playing it long, the payoff is investment and advancement. With playing it safe, the only payoff is discontentment and regret.

I've had opportunities to change my career path, but I've chosen to stay where I am and continue to work at it because I knew that in pursuing other options, I would be settling for less than God's best in my life. The moment you settle for less than God's best is the moment your possibilities become smaller. This is because in settling, you've constricted your mindset to a smaller view of God. You've chosen to believe that the possibilities for your life are limited when, in reality, the possibilities with God are far better than you ever could have dreamed.

One summer I went to watch the sunset out behind the back of our house. I had been driving and saw how beautiful it was. I texted my wife and told her she should come watch it with me. When I met up with her outside, she was commenting on how beautiful it was, but she wasn't even seeing the best part, which was behind the trees she was standing in front of. We walked across the yard and I was able to show her how spectacular it was where the sky really opened up.

Often we settle for seeing less than the best in our lives. We look at an opportunity or a person and say, "Wow, that's beautiful!", but we don't realize God has something even better for us just around the corner. We need to give God the time to lead us to where we can begin to see the many possibilities He has for us. This doesn't mean we are so crippled by fear of making the wrong decision that we don't move forward in any way. This is where the importance of having family and leaders in your life whom you love and trust comes in. Make sure that they know you well and are able to dream big too. Before making a major decision, go to the Lord in prayer and talk with these people. Ask them if they think this is the best direction for you right now and be willing to receive the feedback they give you.

I've thought about why the Israelites were willing to settle for something inferior when they were in the desert. At first it never made sense to me, but the more I thought about it the more I realized they hadn't yet identified with the dream God had given them. Up until this point, they were blindly following Moses. He was the one who had met with God in the burning bush. He had stood before Pharaoh performing the plagues and petitioning for their freedom. Moses had been the one who led them out into the desert and convinced them to trust God before the Red Sea opened up.

Until now, this was a one-man show (with a little help from his brother Aaron), and because of that the Israelites hadn't bought in. God had spoken to Moses about the Promised Land, but the rest of the Israelites hadn't gotten on board or else they would have been able to stay focused on the promise. When God speaks to you and gives you a vision for where He wants you to go, that needs to become your identity – an essential part of who you are and what you do. You need to wear it every day. And just like Moses needed the people to get on board, you need to have others standing with you in faith and agreement.

You weren't called to accomplish God's purposes for your life alone and God hasn't structured His plans in such a way that you could even if you tried. No matter how skilled, talented or anointed you are, you will need the help of others. This is why God has put us in the body of Christ and given us each other. You must surround yourself with godly friends and leaders. But there's another aspect to consider when deciding who will be on your team. The Israelites jumped at the chance to celebrate in the victory, but turned their back on Moses in the face of trials. If someone isn't willing to walk through defeat with you, then they shouldn't be there when you cross the finish line either. Find loyal friends who will walk with you through the good and the ugly.

Unfortunately, the Israelites weren't that kind of people. By now, Moses was more secure in who he was and the position God had given him. When the people complained, his response was, "Your grumbling is not against us but against the Lord" (Exodus 16:18, ESV). He was frustrated with the people, but he no longer was afraid to get "dirty" and keep the people moving toward the dream of inheriting the Promised Land. Stormie Omartian says in her book *The Power of a Praying Wife,* "Dreams don't come true when more time is spent talking about them than praying and working toward achieving them."[1]

The Israelites were content to talk about dreams; in fact, they talked negatively about the dream they were pursuing rather than actually working toward achieving it. They wanted the big dream to come to life *now.* But humans rarely appreciate things that come easy. That's

IF SOMEONE ISN'T
WILLING TO WALK
THROUGH DEFEAT
WITH YOU, THEN
THEY SHOULDN'T BE
THERE WHEN YOU
CROSS THE FINISH
LINE EITHER.

#WHATSNEXTBOOK

why God has called you to start by getting "dirty." As you put in the hard work, the dream will become engraved on your heart. You'll take ownership in it and carry it with pride. You'll believe in it and fight for it with all you've got. You'll become the greatest ambassador of the dream God has given you.

Most of us are familiar with the famous words Dr. Martin Luther King Jr. declared in 1963, "I still have a dream, a dream deeply rooted in the American dream – one day this nation will rise up and live up to its creed, 'We hold these truths to be self evident: that all men are created equal.'"[2] Dr. King was a dreamer who dreamed far bigger than most dare, but he was also not afraid to get "dirty," meaning he wasn't afraid to dig in and do the day-to-day work that was required to move his dreams forward. Prior to his involvement as a civil rights leader, he was carrying out the daily duties of a reverend. But he always knew he wanted to engage the hearts of people and affect social change. As a young man he prayed, "Use me, God. Show me how to take who I am, who I want to be, and what I can do, and use it for a purpose greater than myself."[3]

Eight years before he gave that speech and fourteen years before African Americans were granted full civil rights, he helped lead the Montgomery bus boycott, one of the major catalysts for the Civil Rights Movement. As a leader he led by example, participating in boycotts and sit-ins. He also endured the anger and violence surrounding this cause when his house was bombed and, ultimately, when he was assassinated in 1968. Dr. King knew that this cause was going to be a lengthy one and so he wasn't afraid to get dirty while dreaming big. That dream eventually changed the course of our nation and brought much better conditions for African Americans.

If you're going to dream big, you need to pray hard. That's what Dr. Martin Luther King did. Prayer is the foundation that great dreams are built on, and intense prayer has preceded nearly every major revival in history. One example of great prayers leading to amazing impact is the Ulster Revival in Ireland. In 1857, four men who were new converts to Christianity started gathering in a schoolhouse on Friday nights to study the Bible and pray for their country. At the time, Ireland was plagued by alcoholism, a poor economy, and massive amounts of crime. The tension and violence between Catholics and Protestants was growing to the point where the country was on the brink of a civil war.

In 1858, a man they had been praying for joined their group and by the end of the year there were fifty people coming regularly. Soon after, more than one hundred similar prayer groups had formed across the country meeting in barns, schoolrooms, business places, and homes.

Church services began overflowing and people started meeting in fields and town squares – anywhere they could find a big enough space to congregate. One minister said, "The difficulty used to be to get the people into the church, but the difficulty now is to get them out."[4]

IF YOU'RE GOING TO DREAM BIG, YOU NEED TO PRAY HARD.

Society was incredibly impacted as bars closed and breweries went out of business. Criminal courts convened to find that there were no cases to try and the crime rates plummeted. Shipyard laborers were compelled to honesty and returned tools they had stolen over the years. One company had to build a new storage facility just to hold all the returned tools.

Eventually, the revival spread to Scotland, Wales, and England. Over the course of a year 100,000 souls came to Christ in Ireland. Wales also saw one hundred thousand converts added to the church, which was one tenth of the population. In Scotland, another 300,000 came to Christ. Revival historian Edwin Orr noted that this revival made a greater impact on Ireland than anything known since Patrick took Christianity there.

This incredible movement was still recognized 150 years later in 2008 as David Simpson made a motion in the Northern Irish Assembly to organize events throughout the year to acknowledge "the positive contribution made by the Revival to society" and to recognize "the positive impact that is still felt today."[5] This impact occurred all because four men, hungry for change in their nation, decided to pray.

Moses demonstrated this same kind of fervent prayer. He was in regular communication with God. He knew that his leadership was derived completely from God by listening to what He commanded. Every time a problem came up, the Bible tells us that Moses "cried to the Lord" and then God responded. We see his desire to personally meet with God when he sets aside time to go up on Mount Sinai just to speak with Him. Moses was God's mouthpiece to His people, but to be that mouthpiece, he had to be a great listener. At one point, Moses spent forty days and nights on the mountain meeting, listening, and talking with God.

Moses had a special relationship with God that enabled him to work through the tough situations and continue to advance the people toward obtaining the dream of the Promised Land. There's a section of Scripture that shows just how close he was to God in an exchange at Mount Sinai. All the people were gathered at the foot of the mountain to meet with God as He had instructed. The mountain was surrounded by a cloud of smoke. Thunder and lightning lit up the sky and a loud trumpet blast was heard. The Bible states that in this moment Moses spoke to God and God answered him with thunder. That is the stuff movies are made of.

It's easy for us to think that only people like Moses can have that close of a relationship with God, but we must remember that Moses had all of the same issues we have. He was insecure, didn't speak well, felt unqualified, had trouble with self-control, and was undisciplined at times. In fact, Moses had bigger problems than we do. Don't forget he killed a man!

If after all of that he could still form an incredibly close relationship with God, I'm sure we can do the same. That relationship starts with prayer and reading His words in the Bible.

As you seek God, the dreams He has put in your heart will come to light. And as you continue to pray, those dreams will come to life. But it's important to take note, the cycle of getting dirty and dreaming big needs to regularly repeat itself. I've witnessed leaders who do the work of getting dirty and get to the place where they have achieved big dreams, only to become complacent and see the dream lapse over time to the point where all the work they put in ends with nothing to show for it.

William Booth, founder of the Salvation Army, said, "Prayer must be matched with action. If it is true that Satan trembles when he sees the weakest saint upon their knees … it is also true that Satan trembles much more when, having said his prayers, that same saint rolls up his sleeves and sets out to answer them."

Your prayers will embolden you to dream and drive you to action. As you move forward you'll need to repeat the cycle, because God is constantly moving and creating. He always wants to be taking us to new places of growth in Him. As people made in the image of the Creator, we are designed to be creating. I once heard it said that you start dying the moment you stop dreaming. It's sad to think of life that way, but God created us to always be dreaming because it gives us something to live for and helps Him advance His kingdom.

Each day offers the opportunity to come before God, develop a relationship with Him, and seek Him for the dreams He has given you and how He wants to accomplish them. When you get to the point where you reach a dream, by all means relish it, revel in it, and celebrate what God has done, but don't forget that soon after, you'll be called to get up, dig in, and take the next mountain.

WHO'S YOUR PROVIDER?

As the son of a financial advisor, I'd be remiss to write a book and not talk about finances, especially because the decisions you make about your finances in your early twenties, when you're just starting to manage them on your own, can change the entire course of your life. Decisions like how many loans to take out to pay for school or what house you buy can play an important role in what your finances look like as you go through life. These decisions can also determine your walk with God.

In 2009, when my wife and I decided to leave our regular paychecks behind and begin fundraising by asking people to support us financially, this act challenged many of my preconceived beliefs about God and finances. I had long believed that everything I have comes from God.

My parents had raised me that way, but believing and walking out what you believe are two entirely different things. There was a lot of hard work to be done as we began sending out letters, making hundreds of phone calls, and meeting with potential supporters.

We were working hard to meet a goal in time to move by the date we had determined, but in the midst of all this, God spoke something to me that shifted my perspective. God told me to remember that the pressure to provide isn't mine to take on. He alone is my provider, and so I must learn to trust Him to provide as I carry out the work He has called me to. Without having this understanding, I don't think we would have felt free to take the risks we did and go into full-time ministry.

While my parents had taught me that everything we have comes from God, they had also taught me the value of hard work. I don't disagree with them in this, as the Bible has a lot to say about avoiding laziness. But sometimes we get so caught up in working hard that we see ourselves as the provider instead of God as our provider. You may not realize it, but how you were raised and what you have experienced has already shaped your thinking on money and how you manage your finances.

Your perspective will vary greatly depending on whether you grew up in poverty, a middle class, or a wealthier home. Different people have different ideas of where the lines are drawn to delineate between those categories.

Regardless of numbers, someone who grew up in a home where their parent or parents pinched pennies and struggled to pay the bills each month will view finances much differently than someone who was raised in a home where they got most anything they asked for and never felt in need. Regardless of your experience, there is one truth

SOMETIMES WE GET SO CAUGHT UP IN WORKING HARD THAT WE SEE OURSELVES AS THE PROVIDER INSTEAD OF GOD AS OUR PROVIDER.

that must override all other beliefs you hold. God is your number one provider.

God had to teach this level of trust and reliance on Him to the Israelites as well. In the midst of their grumbling and complaining from lack of food, Moses responded by saying, "At evening you shall know that it was the Lord who brought you out of the land of Egypt, and in the morning you shall see the glory of the Lord ... when the Lord gives you in the evening meat to eat and in the morning bread to the full, because the Lord has heard your grumbling that you grumble against him – what are we? Your grumbling is not against us but against the Lord" (Exodus 16:6-8, ESV).

This time Moses gets it right. He basically tells the Israelites that they have no reason to complain to him because he isn't their provider. Their "beef" was with God since He was the only one who could provide for their needs.

Since Moses never wanted this job in the first place, I'm sure he had decided to take a position of complete reliance on God in all things. Self-reliance would never cut it in his line of work.

While the Israelites had been in slavery, their basic provisions were still taken care of in Egypt. Here in the wilderness with an incredible lack of resources and no way to create them on their own, they would be challenged to rely on God in a way they never had before.Of course, God showed Himself faithful. He rained down bread and quail from heaven each day. I bet you never realized that

God provided the inspiration for *Cloudy with a Chance of Meatballs*, did you?

All jokes aside, God always provides for our needs just as he did for the Israelites. Jesus addressed this when He said:

"I tell you not to worry about everyday life – whether you have enough food and drink, or enough clothes to wear. Isn't life more than food, and your body more than clothing? Look at the birds. They don't plant or harvest or store food in barns, for your heavenly Father feeds them. And aren't you far more valuable to him than they are? Can all your worries add a single moment to your life? And why worry about your clothing? Look at the lilies of the field and how they grow. They don't work or make their clothing, yet Solomon in all his glory was not dressed as beautifully as they are. And if God cares so wonderfully for wildflowers that are here today and thrown into the fire tomorrow, he will certainly care for you. Why do you have so little faith? So don't worry about these things, saying, 'What will we eat? What will we drink? What will we wear?' These things dominate the thoughts of unbelievers, but your heavenly Father already knows all your needs" (Matthew 6:25-32, NLT).

The Psalms tell us that God "owns the cattle on a thousand hills" (Psalm 50:10, NLT). If God knows our needs better than we know them and if everything in the world belongs to Him, then we have no reason to worry or despair. We only need to be diligent workers, stewarding the things He has given us, and then trusting that He will provide all our needs. You need to live like you believe that God is your provider.

When you can grasp that God is your provider and release that pressure from yourself, you experience great freedom and peace of mind. At times when our finances have been tight, I've held to this concept and decided to trust God. I've even said to Him, "God, you are my provider. The pressure is on you to provide, not me." As I've taken that stance, while being diligent and a good steward of what I do have, He has always been faithful to meet all our needs.

Six years ago, Cheryl and I faced a situation that required us to trust God to provide in an unexpected way. We had been working in ministry for less than a year. We were back home visiting family, backing our car out of my mother-in-law's driveway when I shifted into drive. As I pushed the accelerator pedal the engine revved, but nothing happened. I checked again to make sure the car was in drive and, after confirming it was, tried again with the same result. By now I was starting to get frustrated as I knew this was not a sign of anything good. Finally, after trying one more time, the car lurched forward and started moving down the road.

Like anyone else in this situation, all these unsettling thoughts started going through my head. I started thinking What are we going to do? and How much is this going to cost? As we slowed to a stop sign, I looked around at everyone in the car and told them that we needed to stop and pray. Thankfully, we were able to get our car home, but we noticed that the vehicle would jolt any time we reached around 32 miles per hour as the car was shifting through the gears. I was pretty sure I knew what that meant. This car was experiencing an issue with the transmission. This was the same car we had paid $2,000 to replace the transmission in two months before our wedding.

Figuring out that expense had stung then, and I knew it wouldn't be easy now either. I took the car to a mechanic and, sure enough, they reported what I was expecting to hear – the car's transmission was slowly dying. Eventually, we would need to pay to replace the transmission or to buy a new car entirely. Fearing this would be the case, we had been praying about what to do. We had just paid this car off the summer before and in our prayer time we really felt God telling us not to take out another loan. At the same time, we were still trying to reach our funding goals and weren't in any position to pay for a new car, even if it was a clunker.

We knew we had some time to figure things out, as the car was still working for the time being and because it was over the summer there was less travel required for our job. But when we prayed, we also heard God speak, reassuring us that He was our provider and to trust Him alone to provide. As we sought the Lord that summer, we were led to write down a list of what to look for in a new vehicle. We made a list of what we thought God was telling us: 2006 or newer model year (this was in 2010), 60,000 miles or less, good gas mileage, reliable for years to come, and a color my wife would like. I hung the list on our fridge to remind us of what we were praying and believing God for.

But money doesn't just come down from heaven like the bread the Israelites were given, right? Well, we weren't sure how God was going to provide. He didn't tell us that part. We just knew that He was going to, because He has always been and will always be our number one provider.

So, we went through that summer trusting God even when it made us look foolish. We would drive down backroads in our area that were marked 55 miles per hour being sure to go only 30 miles per hour thinking that maybe it just might prolong the life of the transmission if we didn't make it shift through the gears that caused the problem.

I remember laughing together at ourselves and how ridiculous this all was. When family members asked us what we were going to do to fix the car, we would tell them that we were trusting God and we weren't sure yet how our prayers would be answered. They looked at us like we had two heads. One family member upon hearing this replied, "Good luck with that."

Our resolve to take God at His word was paving the way for Him to provide our every need. We could have easily given up and decided we didn't hear God correctly. As months went by, we could have decided it was just too difficult and awkward to keep having those conversations. We could have gone to a car dealership and gotten a loan at any moment. But testimonies of God's goodness aren't derived from choosing the comfortable path. They come from standing in faith on God's promises.

Months passed and we came to the beginning of September. We still didn't have an answer to our situation and we needed to start traveling for our job in just a couple of weeks. One Sunday we were scheduled to speak at a church, but the car started acting odd the night before (more than it had been), and so we called up a person from the church so we could get a ride the next morning. As he drove us to the church, he inquired about our car situation and what was happening. We explained yet again what had been going on and that we were trusting God to provide.

The next morning was Labor Day. I needed to go somewhere, but as I tried to pull out of our apartment parking lot, the car wouldn't move. I climbed the stairs to our apartment feeling discouraged. We had trusted the Lord to provide, even being willing to look foolish to others, and now it seemed like we were at the end of the line. When I told my wife that the car wasn't working, she said something I'll never forget, "Let's begin to praise God for what He's going to do." We turned on some worship music and spent a couple of hours praising God for the provision He was bringing and the car that we would soon have.

That evening I went to check my email and there in my inbox was a message from the man who had taken us to church the day before. He told us that after our conversation the day before, God had impressed on his heart to give us $5,000 toward a new car! In less than 12 hours God had provided an amazing answer through someone we had known for only a couple of months! When you trust God as your number one source, you will never be embarrassed or find yourself lacking. And His provision is far better than you could ever do on your own.

Now, if you know a little bit about cars, you might remember that list we had made and be thinking to yourself, that is not a $5,000 car – which is why the story of God's provision doesn't end here. My grandparents were able to loan us one of their cars as we searched for the perfect replacement.

A few weeks went by and in the meantime, we sold our car on Craigslist for $750. We were having trouble finding a car that fit the specifications we had listed out in prayer. Every night I was scouring websites and during the day we would drive around looking at different car lots. I would try to talk car salesmen down thousands of dollars knowing that I'd never see them again. They didn't like that too much.

One night while searching on Craigslist, I started to pass a listing for a 2006 Hyundai Elantra with 14,000 miles. It was listed for $7,500 and there were no pictures. I was prepared to move on because any car listing on Craigslist without pictures is immediately suspect in my mind. But my wife saw it and stopped me. I tried to explain to her that this car probably was missing an engine or the body was completely totaled. Why else would there be no pictures? "What will it hurt to look into it?" she replied.

I called the phone number listed and quickly found out that the man I was talking to was selling the car for his mother who had just moved into a nursing home. He hadn't been able to take pictures yet and had just thrown the ad up as quickly as possible. The car was in great condition minus a few minor dents and dings, but it was three hours away from our home. Over the phone I talked him down to $5,750 – the exact amount we had and well below the asking price. When I drove out to see the car, I was able to talk him down even a little more. In the end, we bought the car, paid for registration, and fixed all the dents and dings and it was all paid for by the combined money we had received from our friend and selling our broken car.

We had experienced an incredible story of God's goodness, but it was only because we had trusted God, had taken Him at His word, and had chosen to live like we believed God was our provider. The car He provided us was far better than what we could have ever bought on our own. Not only were we able to avoid debt but, when we needed to sell that car three years and 45,000 miles later to upgrade to a van for our growing family, we were also able to sell it for only $150 less than we originally paid for it. Our own efforts could never have worked out that well!

God is the best provider because only He knows exactly what we need. We can see this if we continue reading about the Israelites' situation in the wilderness. The Bible tells us that the Lord instructed the people regarding the manna (bread), "You shall each take an omer (a unit of measure used in ancient times), according to the number of the persons that each of you has in his tent" (Exodus 16:16, ESV). Then it goes on to tell us that everyone gathered according to their house size and that "whoever gathered much had nothing left over, and whoever gathered little had no lack" (Exodus 16:18, ESV).

Furthermore, if anyone gathered more than they had been instructed, it went bad the next morning and was filled with worms. But on the sixth day of the week when they had been instructed to gather a double portion so they could rest on the Sabbath, none of it went bad the next day. God was showing them that they could rest entirely in His provision. Only God knew exactly how much each family needed and made sure to provide the perfect amount.

When we trust Him to provide, we can be assured that we will never be lacking. Resting in God's provision will always exceed our own efforts. This is exactly what my wife and I experienced when we first went into ministry. Though we weren't making as much money as we had hoped, we never lacked as we put our trust in God. Our bills were always paid on time and we never had to go into debt.

One way my wife and I have decided to practically live out the principle of seeing God as our provider is by choosing to never make decisions just because of money. This can be a tough one to stick to when that job opportunity comes up that pays so much better than what you're making now, that price on a house is just too good to pass up, or when you don't really need more clothes, but the store down the street has an amazing sale going on. Sure, there are times that you should take advantage of sales and good deals. That's being a wise steward with your money. But I've heard countless stories of people who were so tempted to make decisions based on money that they now work at jobs they hate, live in homes that severely limit their finances, or have piled up thousands of dollars in credit card debt – all because they made decisions purely motivated by money.

Author Jon Acuff wrote a blog once about a conversation he had with his daughter that changed how he sees money. He was talking with his family over dinner one night about an opportunity that came up. As he shared, his wife said it didn't make sense to take the job as it didn't fit his passions or goals. His immediate response was, "Well, the money is good." Right away his ten-year-old daughter spoke up and said, "Why would you ever do something just for the money? You already have some."[1]

It's easy to get caught up in thinking we don't have enough money, but that's because our perspective about money is usually wrong. We convince ourselves that if we had more money we would have peace, security, significance, and joy. But money can't promise those things. Only God can. Often we attain a certain income level and we're satisfied for a time, only to feel a couple of years later like we've maxed out our finances and once again need more money. When we have a problem, we are more likely to trust money to fix it than we are to trust God.

Why would you ever look to a manmade resource like money to provide for your needs when you know the supernatural God who created the entire universe? You can decide to trust in God as your provider and make decisions based on His leading instead of on what seems to make the most sense financially. You can experience a level of freedom in your finances that most people never realize. You don't need to give in to the rat race mentality that has overtaken American society. You don't need to be paralyzed by fear in your finances and you don't need to let them control your every move. When you let God take the reins and trust Him to provide, you can rest in knowing that He will take care of you and help you make the best decisions with the money He has entrusted to you.

When it comes down to it, the way we view our finances reveals the state of our hearts. God has shown me over the years that if I haven't surrendered my finances to Him, then I haven't fully surrendered my heart to Him. Jesus actually taught this principle in His Sermon on the Mount when He talked about worry, saying, "Where your treasure is, there your heart will be also" (Matthew 6:21, ESV). What we spend our money on reveals what we treasure in life. Pastor Robert Morris, who wrote an incredible book on finances called *The Blessed Life*, puts it this way in one of his sermons on this subject, "When God gets a hold of your heart, He gets a hold of your wallet." You can use your money to show others that you value them, to take care of your family, or yourself. We make decisions about how we spend our money every day, and in turn, make decisions about what we value in life.

I'm not here to make you feel guilty about how you spend your money. Your financial decisions are completely between you and God. What I am speaking to is making sure that you have surrendered your finances completely to Him. God wants us to surrender everything we have to Him because everything we have comes from Him to begin with. Don't worry. Before you start thinking back to my time at the quiet monastery, let me assure you, I'm not calling you to live the life of a monk with only a bed and a Bible to your name. I just want to challenge you to view the money you have and make in a different way than you might have in the past. Once I realized that I needed to surrender my financial decisions to God first and foremost, it changed the way I approached spending my money.

I used to ask myself how my money could benefit me by getting things I wanted. Do you see a pattern there? How *my* money could benefit *me* by getting things *I* wanted. I tithed every week in church (the principle of giving ten percent of your money to the Lord), but I still hadn't fully surrendered my finances to God. I was so wrapped up in myself and my own pleasure that I wasn't asking Him regularly about how I should be spending my money. Once I began talking to God about my finances and asking Him for wisdom on where to spend them, I began to see things differently.

First, I realized that I had been focusing much of my spending on accumulating material things that don't have much worth. The Bible tells us that our material treasures will not pass from this life to the next. I don't know about you, but I'm actually pretty grateful for that. Can you imagine how awful heaven would be if we got to take all our crap with us? We'd be constantly reminded of our geeky high school days when we saw our parents' photo albums or the terrible fashion decisions we made when looking at those clothes we never threw away.

The things we own on earth will not go into eternity, but people will. People are the only thing that will remain after the earth as we know it is gone. So, the good that has been done for the kingdom of God through the use of our treasures will last for eternity. There is no greater investment you make than when you invest into people and the work of God's kingdom.

Not only is God's kingdom an investment that will impact eternity, it is an investment that can be remarkably multiplied as it's passed from one person to the next to the next. Jesus spoke of this in the parable of the sower. He talked about the seeds that when shared with others bore no fruit or were devoured by the enemy, but then He went on to talk about the people who received the words of God and believed saying, "Other seeds fell into good soil and produced grain, growing up and increasing and yielding thirtyfold and sixtyfold and a hundredfold" (Mark 4:8, ESV). Investing your time and finances in the kingdom of God is an investment that can produce thirty, sixty or even a hundred times what you put in. Now that's a wise investment!

That's why I believe that Christians should be the most generous people on the planet. When we view God as our number one source and surrender our finances to Him, generosity should flow out of us because our God is the most generous of all. We see this in the way He gave us His Son, Jesus, without reservation.

Too often the church is seen as a corrupt entity that is only trying to get people's money, but that should never be the case. The church should be using the finances it receives to exhibit incredible generosity and care for the needs of the world.

If you take Jesus at His word and choose not to worry about money, you're less likely to feel a need to keep every penny to yourself. Pastor Robert Morris uses an example in one of his sermons to illustrate how we can have hearts that are always looking to be generous. As he's preaching, he begins to talk about how a thought crossed his mind that he's going out to eat after the service and he doesn't have any cash on him.

Someone at the front of the church quickly stands up and gives him one hundred dollars in cash. Pastor Robert then goes on to explain that the man gave him that money because he had given it to him to hold before the service started. Then he asks the man at the front of the church if he's grieving over that money, but he's not because that money was never his to begin with. It was Pastor Robert's money and the man was just holding it for a little while.

The same is true of our money. We grieve when we give money away because we think it's ours, but the Bible says that the earth is the Lord's and everything in it. Jesus told us that God will give us everything we need. It all comes from Him. And when we see that we're simply borrowing what God has given us, it's much easier to live generously. This is why I've used the word steward to describe our finances at times in this chapter. Because you and I are simply stewards. A steward is a person who manages another's property or financial affairs. We are stewards of what God has given us, and I have decided that out of what God has given to me I will give back to Him.

Maybe as you've been reading this chapter you're feeling overwhelmed or discouraged. Know that it's never too late to start making changes to the way you handle your finances. Even if you've made decisions in the past that you now regret, you still have access to the greatest source you could ever imagine. Whether you're under the weight of thousands of dollars in student loans, wondering how you could ever pay off your credit cards and get out of debt, or stressing over how you will pay the bill that's due tomorrow, God wants to be your provider. Begin living each day believing that He is the best one to provide for you. Start praying about your finances every day, asking Him for wisdom to be a good steward, and looking for ways to be generous.

When I went into ministry and God changed the entire way I viewed money, I never could have dreamed that I would eventually buy a $13,000 van for our family with cash. It's even more incredible that we were able to do this while giving a significant portion of money to a special project at our church. I'm not saying this to brag. We do not live an extravagant lifestyle. We have just learned to be generous and let God take care of the rest. God has blessed our finances because we have put Him first. I know His desire is to bless your finances, too.

As you take these steps of living like you believe that God is your provider, surrendering your finances to Him, and investing into people and the work of God's kingdom, I believe that the promise Jesus gave us will be evident in your life when He said, "Seek first the kingdom of God and His righteousness, and all these things will be added to you" (Matthew 6:33, ESV).

TRUST THE PROCESS

Trust is essential to being a Christian. We've just talked about trusting God with our finances, but to thrive in life, trusting God must be the foundation in every area of our lives. I've found that God regularly gives us opportunities to exercise our faith through choosing to trust Him. As I write this, I'll be turning 31 at the end of this week and we were just blessed with our third child. Our new daughter is beautiful and, overall, a calm and easygoing baby. But having three children under the age of five is a daily exercise in trusting God with our lives.

A couple of days ago, we had a lot of fun getting out and enjoying a beautiful summer day with the family. This morning, after lots of frustration and children constantly disobeying, I was ready to go back to bed by eight o'clock. And it's a Monday.

My wife and I decided to have children because we knew God was telling us to. Some days we have great days with them and we feel like it's worth it. Other days, if I'm being honest, we question why we ever obeyed God. Don't get me wrong, we both love our children even on the worst of days. But some days it's harder to trust that God's plan is the best plan.

We all go through those long, discouraging days, but how we respond makes the difference. My wife Cheryl and I know that the season we're currently in will hopefully be the most challenging one we ever face. Each day we're reminding ourselves that we have to take it one day at a time.

If yesterday was exhausting and frustrating, we have to stay focused to believe that tomorrow could still be great. One bad day doesn't mean every day will be terrible. It's hard to keep that mindset when you're running on little sleep from taking care of a baby in the middle of the night and corralling two very energetic kids during the day.

Life with three children is overwhelming at times, but I know God told me we were supposed to have a third child. And so, even when I don't always feel like God's plan is the best plan, I have to trust that it is. Not only do I need to trust that His plans are best, I need to trust that He loves me and wants good things for my life.

Sometimes we determine to trust God even when things are difficult because we hold to the false idea that being a Christian is all about suffering. We mistakenly think if we're suffering enough, then we're living for Christ. While the Bible makes it clear that being a Christian will include suffering and sacrifice, I don't believe that God is up in heaven dreaming up more ways for us to be miserable. Following His ways instead of the world's ways will be difficult at times – incredibly difficult actually.

We may even suffer at times, yet we are promised that obedience also brings rewards. God told the Israelites that they would be blessed if they obeyed Him, but I don't obey God just because I'll be blessed. I obey Him because I love Him and out of that love I know I can trust Him.

As I grow older, I feel like life is one really long trust fall. Do you remember doing those when you were younger? If you were in a church youth group, it's almost a guarantee that you participated in a trust fall at one time or another because youth pastors love to subject naive teenagers to random acts of stupidity that we all laugh at later and wonder what our parents were thinking trusting a guy with a trendy haircut who barely graduated college with their children's lives.

In a trust fall, someone stands on a chair or table with their arms folded across their chest and leans back while completely trusting a couple of friends below to put their arms out and catch them. Or at least that's how it was supposed to work. But you always had that one "friend" who thought it was funny to drop you while nearly cracking your head open on the tile floor below. I'm sure you weren't that guy or girl.

Life can feel like one really long trust fall. I can think that I'm someone who has really gotten good at trusting God, only to be put in a situation where I realize I'm still growing in my ability to trust.

Even though it's cliché to say, life is a process filled with ups and downs, twists and turns, and various unexpected detours. While it may be counterintuitive, we must trust the process that God is working in our lives.

Moses and the Israelites had to trust God in every step of the process He was taking them through. But Joshua, who served under Moses, must have really struggled with trusting God's process.

Joshua was born in Egypt prior to the Israelites escaping, was selected by Moses to lead them in their first battle after leaving Egypt, and accompanied Moses when he climbed Mount Sinai to receive the Ten Commandments from God. Moses had identified Joshua as a promising young leader and was grooming him for the future.

Once Aaron lost control of the people and let them make a golden calf to worship, he must have been a shoo-in to become Moses' new right hand man. I'm sure Joshua was feeling pretty great about the direction things were headed. He probably dreamed of the day he could lead God's people into the Promised Land.

The problem was that the Israelites were stubborn and averse to listening to God. What should have been a triumphant entry into the abundant land God had promised was delayed 40 years because of disobedience. Even Moses got in on the act when God told him to speak to a rock so that water would come out of it and, instead, out of frustration, he hit the rock. This one act of disobedience ensured that he would miss out on seeing the Promised Land.

In fact, Joshua and Caleb were the only two men who came out of Egypt and lived to enter the Promised Land. So, as Joshua was waiting for his turn, waiting for the process to play out the way God had assured that it would, you can imagine waiting wasn't easy.

God was taking the Israelites through a very long process to get them where they needed to be, one that was so lengthy it wouldn't reach its completion until an entire generation had passed away. But through it all, Joshua continued to trust in God's goodness.

When Moses sent 12 spies to survey the Promised Land, Joshua and Caleb were the only two who returned with a good report and encouraged the people to take the land because God had given it to them. The people, overcome by fear and unable to trust God, relented and instead complained again that God had led them into the wilderness only to let them die.

That must have been a hard day for Joshua. Actually, it was probably a hard couple of decades, especially knowing that it was someone else's disobedience that cost him. And yet, Joshua continued to trust the process. He continued to serve the Lord and Moses, which eventually paid off.

In the book of Proverbs we're instructed to "trust in the Lord with all our hearts and lean not on our own understanding" (Proverbs 3:5, ESV). Those are great words of wisdom and people quote this verse often, but have you ever found those words to be much harder to live out when you're facing a trial? Sometimes words, no matter how uplifting and encouraging, feel like mere words when you're staring despair in the face.

When you've lost your fifty-year-old parent to cancer or you can't find a job that pays more than minimum wage when you have a family to support or when your marriage of two years ends in divorce, then those words suddenly seem weak. How are you supposed to trust that God is a good Father who has incredible plans for your life when you're going through a hurricane of emotions and loss?

How was it that Joshua was able to trust God when he had done all the right things, but was now left to wander the desert for forty years? How are we to trust the process when all we feel is complete anguish?

I think that Joshua was able to trust God even in the midst of incredible discouragement because of what he had learned of who God was. He had lived through so much as God delivered the Israelites time and time again. Over and over Moses had modeled for him the act of trusting God even when their situation seemed hopeless.

What Moses said as the Israelites stood up against the Red Sea with the Egyptian army bearing down on them showed the depths of what God had done in Moses' heart since he went into Egypt to free the people. In that moment, instead of getting worried or anxious, Moses told the people this simple truth, "Do not be afraid ... The Lord will fight for you, you need only to be still" (Exodus 14:13-14, NIV).

Making a statement like that when you're in the kind of situation he was in taught Joshua that trusting God is always the best course of action. And when God affirmed Moses' trust by splitting open the Red Sea, it was a moment Joshua could never forget.

Joshua had milestone moments in his life that he could look back on to see God's handiwork. And, you might not realize it, but you have those moments as well. They probably aren't memories of an evil king being attacked by giant locusts or walking across Lake Michigan on dry ground.

I'm sure you can remember times where God showed Himself faithful in your life, whether it was when you prayed for that A on a test or when you saw your grandmother recover from an illness. They might feel like small anchors to hold onto, but if you grab hold of them and choose to "lean not on your own understanding," you will see that God is worthy of your trust.

When it comes down to it, we won't always feel like trusting God, but He will always be the tether we can hold onto that will pull us through the process because the Bible follows up the instruction of trusting in the Lord with all your heart with a promise to those who do it.

Isaiah tells us that, "Those who trust in the Lord will find new strength. They will soar high on wings like eagles. They will run and not grow weary. They will walk and not faint" (Isaiah 40:31, NLT). We must take hold of that promise because trusting in God will always produce far better results than we could on our own.

Toby is another missions director who works with young people that I interviewed for this book. He put it this way, "A day of God's power is worth more than one hundred years of your best effort." Moses and Joshua could definitely vouch for that with all they saw God do. You may not know where the road will lead when you put your trust in God, but you'll find joy in the process as you learn more about who He is. And if you commit to let God take you through His process for your life, the end result will far outweigh the challenge it takes to walk through it.

How Cheryl and I started dating is the perfect example. We met in ninth grade. I had gone to a Christian school my whole life and this was my first time setting foot in a public school. Awkward and unsure of what to expect, Cheryl and I sat near each other in our first two classes each morning. While I'm a very talkative person, I didn't say much for the first few months as I was trying to figure out my place in this completely new environment. Because my last name starts with the letter "Z" I sat in the last row with the students who needed special attention and were assigned teacher's aides. My timidity combined with my seat location actually caused Cheryl to assume that I was one of the students in need of an aide.

After some time passed, she and I got into various conversations and eventually she realized that I was normal, actually she must have considered me something much more than normal, because she soon found herself attracted to me. I started to pick up on this and eventually she revealed to me her feelings. Unfortunately, I was not

A DAY OF GOD'S POWER IS WORTH MORE THAN ONE HUNDRED YEARS OF YOUR BEST EFFORT.

as interested in her at first. I regret that I wasn't good at letting her down gently and said some things I later had to apologize for. When it came down to it though, she wasn't a Christian and I had made a commitment to only date Christians. I told her just that, making sure my intentions were quite clear.

A few months passed and I began to take an interest in one of her best friends. However, this friend was also not a Christian and when I confessed to Cheryl my interest, she made sure to remind me of the commitment I had made. God has an incredible sense of humor. He can speak to you through people who don't even know they are hearing His voice. And so, being convicted by someone who clearly had her own motives, I moved on.

A year passed and Cheryl started coming to church and attending our youth group. By now I had gone out of my way in the not-so-nicest of terms to make it abundantly clear that I wasn't interested in Cheryl. I'm fairly certain if given the chance to do a trust fall in youth group, she would have chosen to move and let me fall to incur some form of injury.

Before you start hating me, please remember that we all do and say stupid things in high school. Through all of this, for some unknown reason, Cheryl continued to hold feelings for me. She actually told me later that she was sure God had told her I was to be her husband. In the fall of our sophomore year, she attended a youth conference and gave her life to Jesus.

Over the next few months I saw the transformation that took place in her life. I saw that she was taking her relationship with God seriously. It was evident she hadn't made this decision for me, but truly it was a decision she had made for herself. At this point I still didn't feel anything more than friendship for her. Then one day we planned to walk around her neighborhood with friends to raise money for the 30 Hour Famine.

This is an event youth groups participate in to raise money and awareness for world hunger. When Cheryl and I met up for the event, only one other friend was able to come and it turned out to be just the three of us.

We decided to go anyway and, over the course of the next few hours, we began to laugh, have fun, and eventually Cheryl and I began to flirt with each other. It was totally unexpected on my part. A few days later while lying in bed I began to realize that I had never prayed and asked God what He thought about Cheryl and me being in a relationship. I decided to pray about it and as I did I suddenly became certain that I was supposed to ask her out.

What I didn't realize was that at the same time I was praying, she was hanging out with her girlfriends who were encouraging her to give up on the idea of dating me. They convinced her that she had wasted too much time and energy hoping this would all work out.

She promised them that she was done with me and that even if I asked her out she would say no. But God's process hadn't been completed yet, and all those years she had spent trusting His process had led to this moment.

The next day I asked her if we could start dating. Of course, she was completely caught off guard. She began to grill me on my motives and asked me if I felt sorry for her. Once I convinced her that was not the case, she decided to forgo that promise she had made to her friends and said yes.

Now here we are, three kids and ten years of marriage later. In total we've been dating over half our lives! I'm so thankful that Cheryl had the faith, even before she completely understood it, to trust the process God had ordained for our lives. I couldn't imagine life without her or without our children.

There's no way I could have ever dreamed that I would find the woman I would marry in the way that I did. Our story is one of the reasons why I know that trusting God's plan will always be the best plan. God's plans don't usually play out the way we would want or picture them to, but they always lead to an outcome far better than we ever could have dreamed.

There's a Bible verse in the book of Isaiah where God says, "My thoughts are not your thoughts, neither are your ways my ways … For as the heavens are higher than the earth, so are my ways higher than your ways and my thoughts than your thoughts" (Isaiah 55:8-9, ESV). If you've been around church people enough, you'll hear these verses quoted often. It's a great portion of Scripture. I've been known to quote these verses myself quite a few times, but they're even more effective if we look at prior verses that serve as a way of setting these up.

Earlier in this passage Isaiah implores us to listen diligently and incline our ears to what God is going to say. He says that if we will respond in this way our souls will live, God will make an everlasting covenant with us and have mercy on us. That's quite encouraging coming from an Almighty God who could do whatever He wants with us and who goes on to speak of the difference and distance between us and Him. But it starts with being an active listener. The best means we have for trusting Him in His ways is by inclining our ears, hearing from Him, and then surrendering our hearts to whatever He has for our lives.

It's when we incline our ears and hear from Him that we can center our minds on His truth and combat any fear that would discourage us from trusting Him. We won't always get neatly wrapped answers as to why God does the things He does or lets the things happen that happen, but because we are human there will be times that you aren't able to understand every question life poses. I've decided to be OK with that because I can't expect to know everything and, even if it were possible, I'm not sure I'd want that kind of responsibility.

Trusting Him in all times and situations is far from easy. It may not even feel worth it sometimes. But I've seen the difference in outcomes between those who trust in God and those who don't. I've seen the hope that God gives in the midst of a storm, and I've seen the despair that overtakes those who don't have Him. But to trust

Him, you must take the first step. That's how beginning a relationship with Christ works, taking the first step in trusting Him, and that's how it continues – one moment of trusting Him at a time. As you take that first step, you'll see that one act of trust produces more trust.

The progression of trust is often like a snowball rolling downhill. It begins with something small and then gathers momentum as you see God's faithfulness time and time again until, at last, you're able to trust Him for incredible victories. For Moses it started with trusting a voice in a fiery bush and then snowballed until he was trusting God to pull back the waters of an entire sea. For me, it began with saying a prayer and giving him my life at three years old and it snowballed until I found myself leaving behind a job and my hometown to set out on a new adventure that would lead me into my calling. Now, I know that God is real and that I can trust Him because of what I've seen Him do in my life.

When you choose to listen to His voice and then take the first step of faith, the snowball starts rolling. Before you know it, you'll find that not only are you unshaken by the small things that used to bother you, but you don't even sweat the big stuff. This is the only way we were able to trust God to provide when we faced those problems with the transmission in our car. We had built up faith over time as we trusted God in our small situations, and now we could trust Him with a problem that seemed far more daunting. Faith is knowing that everything will work out even when our circumstances don't currently line up with what God's Word has promised. Faith is choosing to take God at His word instead of worrying.

When we try to do things ourselves, we rob God of the joy He gets from proving His faithfulness. Our faith gives God the opportunity to prove His faithfulness. And it's amazing to see His faithfulness in action because it goes so far beyond what we could ever accomplish on our own. I've heard it said that you can have as little as you are satisfied with or as much as God wants to give you.

Only as your faith gathers momentum can you find the confidence to lean into God's providence as if falling into the arms of someone you knew would always catch you. It's the only trust fall where you never need to worry about the outcome. Choose to listen diligently and believe that His plans will always be the best plans. Trust the process. You won't be disappointed.

KEEP YOUR PERSPECTIVE ON THE PROMISE

A s I mentioned in the last chapter, we recently had our third child. You'd think after having two children, you'd feel like a pro at the whole pregnancy thing. Sure, you've got more figured out and a better idea of what to expect than the first time you went through it, but the problem is that every pregnancy can be completely different. Each pregnancy my wife has gone through has presented its own share of challenging side effects, but this pregnancy was the most difficult.

We discovered she was pregnant in November. While we were thinking we would have a third child, the timing was quite the surprise. The next four months were filled with one challenge after another.

Our four-year-old daughter saw a movie that scared her right before Christmas. So, while we were visiting my mother-in-law, our daughter woke up all throughout the night on Christmas Eve crying and frightened from bad dreams. It made for a quite tiring Christmas Day and almost ruined the experience for all of us.

A week later our kids got sick, which caused us to ring in the New Year by ourselves. As someone who is an extrovert and loves to be around people for the holidays, I was feeling quite depressed. Thankfully, I had made a conscious decision on Christmas Day to set aside how tired and grumpy I was feeling and, frankly wanted to be, to have a good perspective and just enjoy time with my family. I felt like the Lord encouraged me and gave me peace, knowing that life would be more enjoyable if I was able to keep the right perspective.

I'm glad He revealed that to me on Christmas Day, because unfortunately things only got harder. A couple of weeks later my dad and two brothers came to go skiing and snowboarding. We've been doing this for years without any incidents, but this time my younger brother fell and hit his head. After towing him down the mountain and having him evaluated, we took him to a nearby hospital where we were told he had suffered a concussion.

The next day we found out my wife had come down with shingles. If you've never encountered them before, shingles are like chicken pox on steroids that affect your nerves and cause a terribly painful burning in the affected parts of your body.

Usually only people over the age of 50 get them, but here she was trying to fight through them while still in her first trimester of pregnancy, which meant she couldn't take any medication.

A month later, while she was still fighting off the shingles, our whole family contracted a terrible stomach bug. This was the first time both my wife and I have been sick while the kids were also sick. Picture no sleep, feeling like you're going to constantly lose your lunch out of both ends, and then having to comfort and clean up after two little ones who are going through the same thing. Not fun.

Have you ever been in one of those seasons where you feel like everything is coming against you? Now before you go thinking that this chapter is just going to be one long pity party, I'm not telling you all these things so you can feel bad for me. Although, if you don't, I question if you are more cold than Elsa from *Frozen*. OK, give me a break with that reference, I'm a father to two daughters. I'm telling you these things because I want to share with you how God helped us get through this challenging season and what He taught us during this time.

When we encountered these challenges, I had to set my heart and mind on God. I had to decide to place my trust in God and remember that even in the midst of trying times He is good. I wasn't forcing myself to be positive, but rather I was forcing myself to focus on God first and foremost and the result was that I was more positive in the face of trials. Our perspective greatly influences how we view our lives and the course we ultimately take.

When Joshua and Caleb were the only two spies to come back from the Promised Land with a good report, it was because they had the right perspective and were able to stay focused on what God had told them. We can see two very different perspectives in the way that Joshua and Caleb viewed their mission and how the other 10 spies viewed their chances of taking the land God had called them to. Part of the problem with their perspective was that Moses misled them. When God told Moses to send out the spies, He said, "Send out for yourself men so that they may spy out the land of Canaan, which I am going to give to the sons of Israel; you shall send a man from each of their fathers' tribes, every one a leader among them" (Numbers 13:2, NASB).

When Moses sent them to spy out the land of Canaan, he added quite a bit to God's original instructions saying to them, "See what the land is like, and whether the people who live in it are strong or weak, whether they are few or many. How is the land in which they live, is it good or bad? And how are the cities in which they live, are they like open camps or with fortifications? How is the land, is it fat or lean? Are there trees in it or not? Make an effort then to get some of the fruit of the land" (Numbers 13:18-20, NASB).

Moses sends them out and he tells them to look for all these things. Then Moses instructs them to see whether the land is good or bad. Notice that when the Lord spoke, He only told Moses to send the men out to spy out the land. He didn't tell him to have them look for all these other things. Have you ever done that in your life where you add things on that God didn't tell you to? For example, you believe God is challenging you to read your Bible more, but then you decide it has to be two chapters a day and you have to spend an hour in prayer as well. Before you know it, you feel overwhelmed and can't make it through one week!

On top of adding onto God's instructions, it's clear that Moses is already questioning God's promise when he tells them to determine whether the land is good or bad. God had told him back at the burning bush that He was taking them to a land flowing with milk and honey. This was God's way of telling Moses that it was going to be a great home for the Israelites. God had also told him that wherever he set his feet would be Israel's land. He speaks to Moses right here and refers to the Promised Land as that "which I am going to give to the sons of Israel" (Numbers 13:2, NASB). But Moses didn't keep his perspective on the promise.

It's when the spies started looking around at the things Moses had told them to look for, not the things God had told them to look at, that fear and confusion began to set in. And before you get all frustrated with Moses and the Israelites, think about yourself for a minute. How often do we look at our situations and let fear and confusion blind us from what God has said? My wife and I have struggled with this a number of times.

When she was going through this pregnancy with our third child, she began to have times where her heart would start racing out of nowhere. Cheryl is a pretty calm person and this was completely out of the norm for her. While we didn't want to jump to any conclusions and thought it possibly was just something related to pregnancy hormones, when you're experiencing issues with your heart, you don't mess around.

At her appointment with her doctor, she shared about what she had been experiencing and the concerns we had. The doctor immediately scheduled an appointment for her with a cardiologist specialist. The day came for her appointment and she was really nervous. What would the doctor say and how would she respond? She sat down in the waiting room and noticed that she was the only person there under the age of 50. She thought to herself, What am I doing here? She was called in and the nurses asked questions and ran various tests to see what was going on. They sent her home with a monitor to wear for a couple of days and then send back. The readings from this monitor would give them a better idea of what was happening.

About a week later, she went in again to review the results from the monitor with a doctor. When he came in the room, the first thing he said to her was, "Cheryl, you have the healthiest heart I'm going to see all year." She took a deep breath, feeling relieved. He went on to explain that it must have been pregnancy hormones and that nothing from the test results showed any abnormalities. In fact, her heart was incredibly strong. He showed her the healthy number of times her heart had beat in the 24 hours she had been wearing the monitor.

When she read that number as she digested this good news, God whispered in her ear, "Cheryl, I knew that number." It was as if God was telling her that there was never anything to worry about. He knows exactly how many times her heart beats just like the Bible tells us that He knows the exact number of hairs on our head. When we keep our perspective on Him, we never need to worry about the challenges we face. We never need to let fear and confusion cloud the promises He's given us like the fearful, confused report the 10 spies gave.

When the 10 spies came back from checking out the land, this is what they said, "We went in to the land where you sent us; and it certainly does flow with milk and honey, and this is its fruit" (Numbers 13:27, NASB). Notice how they said, "We went in to the land where *you* sent us" (emphasis mine). They were talking to Moses and this sentence shows the mistake they made in this process. They saw this as a mission from a man, not from God. It's no wonder their report was given from a human perspective and not God's perspective.

After they talked about how great the land was, they went on to say, "Nevertheless, the people who live in the land are strong, and the cities are fortified and very large; and moreover, we saw the descendants of Anak there" (Numbers 13:28, NASB). The descendants of Anak were giants who lived in the land of Canaan at that time. "Nevertheless" means despite all of that. At that moment, Moses, and every man of faith in Israel should have cried out and said, "Nevertheless nothing! How can one say, 'We went to the land, found it good, and God's promise true,' and then say, 'Despite all this …'"?

Essentially what these spies were saying was, "Despite God's faithful promise, the people who dwell in the land are strong. Despite God's faithful promise, the cities are fortified and very large. Despite God's faithful promise, we saw the descendants of Anak there."

What they could have been saying was, "The people who dwell in the land are strong, but because of God's faithful promise we are stronger. The cities are fortified and very large, but because of God's faithful promise we will win the victory. The descendants of Anak live there, but because of God's faithful promise we can defeat them."

They did not keep their perspective on the promise or else they would have had full confidence in what God had told them. Just as when the spies saw all those things in the land, or when my family went through those incredibly challenging months, sometimes it seems like everything is against us, but we must hold onto the promise God has given us. God's promise always triumphs over any obstacle.

God's Word tells us that He is the same yesterday, today and forever. Not only that, but we are also told that He cannot break a promise. He would not be a perfect, holy, and truthful God if He were to break His promises.

A number of years back I read something from author Beth Moore in her book *Praying God's Word* that really stood out to me. She wrote, "As long as our minds rehearse the strength of our stronghold more than the strength of our God, we will be impotent (powerless)."[1]

Have you been rehearsing the strength of your stronghold, more than the strength of your God? Are you looking at your giants through a human perspective or God's perspective? Joshua and Caleb were the only two spies who remained focused on God's strength.

We're told that Caleb quieted the people and said, "We should by all means go up and take possession of it, for we will surely overcome it" (Numbers 13:30, NASB). Joshua and Caleb believed and trusted what the Lord had said.

They took God at His word that He had promised them the land. And because of this, they were not afraid to confront the giants in the land. But the other spies believed in what they saw in the natural instead of what was promised in the supernatural.

Of those spies, only Joshua and Caleb survived to see the Promised Land. In fact, Moses died beforehand, too. God had to wipe out the spirit of unbelief in Israel.

God has already promised you the victory. You just have to see it through His perspective instead of yours. All these spies saw the same things in Canaan, but they saw them through different perspectives.

When you feel like everything is coming against you and you are discouraged, will you choose to think like Joshua and Caleb or like the other spies? Will you look at the problems you face in the natural or remember the God who operates in the supernatural? Joshua chose to remember that God operates in the supernatural.

After Moses died, Joshua took his place as the leader of Israel and God gave him the opportunity to take the Promised Land. I'm sure Joshua clearly remembered the mistakes that had been made the first time around. So, there were three things that Joshua did differently.

First, he took God at His word. God spoke to Joshua and told him that He would be with Joshua wherever he went. Unlike Moses, he trusted that God would do as He promised. He chose to walk by faith and not by sight. He trusted that God loved His people and wanted to provide a good place for them, even if it looked impossible. You need to trust that God loves you and wants to take care of you. You must take Him at His word.

Open your Bible and meditate on verses that have stood out to you, remember the things He's spoken to you in your quiet times with Him, and review any prophetic words you've gotten over the years. Write out those Bible verses, lines from worship songs, or encouraging quotes and place them around the house so you're regularly reminded of His words.

God wants to speak to you, and you can trust that when He does speak He knows what's best for you. His words are a powerful tool in our lives for direction and guidance. After all, it's by His words that the whole earth was created. The words He's spoken to you haven't changed.

Second, Joshua removed the extra voices. He sent spies into the land again, but this time instead of sending 12, he sent just two. Do you think it's a coincidence that last time only two spies came back with a good report and this time Joshua only sent two? This time they came back saying, "The Lord has surely given the whole land into our hands;

all the people are melting in fear because of us" (Joshua 2:24, NIV).

When you're going through a challenge or you're believing God for a supernatural miracle, there will be plenty of doubters who want to speak up and speak into your life. But you need to remove the extra voices. Don't block everyone out, because that's not healthy. But choose to listen only to the closest family and leaders who know you best and who you know have your best in mind. Remove the extra voices of those who are always sowing words of discouragement. Ignore the voices of those who try to discourage you from what God has promised you.

Lastly, Joshua went into the Promised Land with praise. When it was time to take Jericho, God instructed the people to march around the city walls blowing trumpets and praising Him. In those days they often sent the worship leaders into battle before the rest of the army. Can you imagine your hipster worship pastor leading the charge into Jericho with his rolled up skinny jeans and French press? That's a funny picture, and yet, God had communicated to His people that worship is what wins our battles.

You can keep your perspective on the promise by starting every day with praise and then continuing that throughout your day when you pray for meals or listen to music at your desk. I often begin thanking God for another day to live when I first wake up or I'm in the shower. I want my mind to be centered on thankfulness from the moment I open my eyes. My wife and I have seen that our family can be having a terrible day, and we notice a significant difference when we listen to worship music.

There is one distinction I should make here. I'm not calling us to thank God *for* everything. I'm calling us to thank God *in* everything. There will be situations and trials you face in life that will be extremely hard. There will be times when the things coming against you are not sent by God. You shouldn't thank God for those things. But through it all, you can still thank God for who He is and His grace to help you persevere and come out the other side.

That's why our perspective is so important. The difference between the person who is defeated and the person who is victorious is their perspective. Our natural human perspective says, "What has God done for me?" But someone with the right perspective says, "What has God promised me?" Remember, your life and the things you are called to are a mission from God, not from man. If you're going to be successful on this mission, you'll need to think in a way that is different from how you normally think.

The 12 spies all saw the same things in Canaan. But they saw them through different perspectives. Two of them, Joshua and Caleb, were able to think differently about the challenge in front of them. Will you choose to think like Joshua and Caleb or like the other spies? Are you viewing your trials through a human perspective or God's perspective? It's amazing how different your situation can look when viewed in the right light.

THE DIFFERENCE BETWEEN THE PERSON WHO IS DEFEATED AND THE PERSON WHO IS VICTORIOUS IS THEIR PERSPECTIVE.

In 2016, former NBA player and Oklahoma City Thunder coach Monty Williams suffered a tragic loss when his wife was killed in a head-on collision after a woman crossed over the center line. In the midst of this terrible situation it was incredible to hear what Monty shared at her funeral.

He began by saying the kinds of things you would expect to hear at a funeral, "This is hard for my family, but this will work out … It doesn't mean it's not hard. Doesn't mean it's not painful." But then he continued by sharing a perspective that could only come from someone who has chosen to trust God no matter what happens.

He said, "Let's not lose sight of what's important. God will work this out. My wife is in heaven…. When we walk away from this place today, let's celebrate. Because my wife is where we all need to be…. We didn't lose her. When you lose something you can't find it. We know exactly where my wife is…. God is important. What Christ did on the cross is important…. Let's keep what's important at the forefront."[2]

That is an incredible perspective in the face of unspeakable tragedy. Honestly, I'm not sure I'd be able to say those words in a time like that. But as Christians we have something that the rest of this world doesn't have.

We have a hope in Jesus Christ that can help us persevere when others are crushed. We have a joy that can carry us when nothing makes sense. We have a God who can comfort us in times of sorrow.

So, when it seems like everything is coming up against you, keep your perspective on the promise. When you lose your job unexpectedly and you don't know how you will pay the bills, keep your perspective on the promise. When you have a miscarriage and feel hopeless, keep your perspective on the promise. When your spouse brings you divorce papers, keep your perspective on the promise. When you find out you have cancer, keep your perspective on the promise. When a loved one passes away, keep your perspective on the promise.

God's promise always triumphs over any obstacle. Keep your eyes fixed on Him.

GO! TAKE THE LAND

We've covered a lot in our time together, but now it's time to put action to what you've learned. Just as Joshua spent time learning under Moses and eventually there came a time for him to step up and lead the Israelites into the Promised Land, it's time for you to go take the land that God is calling you to.

Hopefully as you've read through this book, sought the Lord, and talked with people you trust, you've begun to get a better understanding of God's plans for your life. You may not feel like you have the complete picture yet. That's OK! In fact, it's rare that it works that way. God didn't give the Israelites the Promised Land all at once, but little by little. He knew that they weren't prepared to handle getting it all at one time. That's why God didn't tell them to take the entire Promised Land right away. He just told them to march on one city – Jericho. Every victory in life begins with one step of faith.

It was when Moses took a step of faith and went back to Egypt that God's people were delivered out of slavery. It was when Caleb and Joshua put the unbelief of the past generation behind them and took the step of faith necessary to go defeat Jericho that God's favor was revealed. As you take the first steps of faith God has spoken to you after you've read this book, His favor will go before you as well.

I've seen this at work in my own life. As I took these steps of faith that I've shared with you – cultivating my relationship with God, blooming where I'm planted, trusting Him and fighting fear – God's favor has gone before me. As I've been writing this book, the position of executive director that I was turned down for before opened up, and this time I was chosen for the job. I truly believe this is a result of trusting God and seeking His will in every area of my life. Trusting Him throughout this process was not easy, but it brought great reward and I'm now prepared to go take the land He has given me.

God's faithfulness is incredible. He uses broken people like Moses, Joshua, and even me and you to accomplish amazing things. And God has called you to greater things than you realize. He has been writing your story from before you were born, and He has great plans for your life. You may have tried to direct the story yourself at times. At other times you may have felt like you were just observing your story as life happened around you, but now with God's help you can live your story to the fullest.

While it's tempting to think that your story isn't great because it's not filled with great exploits yet, let me assure you that your story is just getting started and the best is yet to come. You have decades of fruitfulness ahead of you. Don't allow yourself to succumb to the pitfalls we've discussed, like the comparison game or impatience. Make the investments in your life now that will launch your future. You may feel as if no one sees your efforts right now, but you can trust that God does.

It would have been easy for Joshua to throw in the towel when no one was willing to listen to him and Caleb, but it was Joshua's faithfulness to God when the spies first went into the Promised Land that was the catalyst for his future victory. Don't give up! Your victory is ahead of you. Don't let anyone discourage you and don't let the enemy of your soul lie to you.

God created you with a purpose and if you listen to His voice, you will succeed even if it seems like everything is stacked against you. Moses should have died when Pharaoh issued a decree to kill all the Israelite boys, and again when he murdered the Egyptian, but God's plan couldn't be stopped, not by a king and not even by the very person He had chosen to accomplish it through. When we study the Bible, we see this same story time and time again.

Joseph should have been killed or at least held captive as a slave his whole life, but God used him to save a nation. David committed the sins of adultery and murder, but still God chose to redeem the world through his bloodline. Jonah turned his back on God and should have died inside the belly of a fish, and yet God gave him a second chance to save the people of Nineveh from destruction. The list goes on and on. Even the Bible's main character appeared to be utterly defeated until He won the victory over death and sin three days later!

When I think through this list, I'm reminded of the book of Hebrews where the author talks about all the famous people in the Bible who have prevailed by faith. It speaks of heroes like Abraham, Moses, David and even Rahab, the prostitute. Then it says this in the next chapter: "Therefore, since we are surrounded by such a great cloud of witnesses, let us throw off everything that hinders and the sin that so easily entangles. And let us run with perseverance the race marked out for us" (Hebrews 12:1, NIV).

We don't exactly know who wrote the book of Hebrews, but whoever it was, I love the imagery the author uses here when he compares life to a race that we're running. It's easy when you're young to think that you've missed out on something – that the race has already passed you by. It's cliché, but I'm going to say it anyway. Life is not a one hundred meter dash; it feels much more like a marathon. It's an exhausting, up and down, takes everything from you and requires all you have, kind of race. And the only ones who finish well are those who rely on faith in God.

You see, all of us are running. Some just don't know what they're running for. As Christians, we know the reason why we're running this race. We know the impact we can have on the world because Jesus has shown us in His example and called us to join in with Him.

Every once in a while, usually after a period of indulging too much in ice cream and my wife's baking,

I take up running again. It's not something I enjoy at all. Usually I prefer something competitive like basketball or racquetball to motivate me to exercise. I have a friend who loves running, though. She has done a number of 5K's and half marathons and hopes to participate in a marathon some day.

One day as I was telling her about my lack of motivation for running and how I enjoy competition more, she encouraged me to start finding ways to compete against myself when I run. She talked about trying to beat my times or taking routes that had more hills. I had been doing this a little already, but once she explained it a certain way, I began taking it to heart.

Each time I would try to beat my last time, and I was seeing success. Steadily my times went down, one minute this time, then another two minutes the next. I was challenging myself to be better and the result was that I was more engaged, and I was running far faster than I thought possible.

I want to challenge you to think of your daily race in the same way. How can you do today better than yesterday? Maybe for you it's spending five more minutes with God in the morning, or setting a bigger goal when you work out, or being more committed at work. Whatever it is for you, challenge yourself to run the race stronger and take on greater challenges than you did the day before. We've talked a little bit about the unhealthy comparison game, so don't get into competing against others. Keep the focus on being a better you each day.

KEEP THE FOCUS ON BEING A BETTER YOU EACH DAY.

Run the race with perseverance and see what God does. As you hold onto the promises of God, your race is unfolding. As you remain faithful, your story of certain victory is being written. There's quite a while before you cross that finish line, which gives you plenty of time to recover if you get tripped up. Don't let anything hold you back from taking new ground each day.

The best part is, while others are trying to run the race of life and win on their own, you are not alone. The beginning of that verse in the book of Hebrews says we are surrounded by this great cloud of witnesses. That's referring to all the heroes of the faith who were just listed in the chapter before this. How incredible it is to think of people like Abraham, Moses, Joshua, David, Elijah and so many others we've read about cheering us on from heaven! Their stories began with a step of faith and now they're encouraging us to take that step.

On top of that, your God is fighting for you, and His heart is to see you run with strength and endurance. He's running with you every step of the way. When you feel like you can't go any farther, He'll pick you up and carry you. When you get anxious and worry about whether you're doing enough, His peace will steady you. He loves you and He has everything you need.

Now is the time to step out in faith. It's time to conquer fear and insecurity. It's time to pursue what God has called you to. You've got all of heaven cheering you on. It's time to go and take the land!

NOTES

Chapter 1

1. Natalie Wolchover, "FYI: How Many Different Ways Can a Chess Game Unfold?," *Popular Science*, December 15, 2010, http://www.popsci.com/science/article/2010-12/fyi-how-many-different-ways-can-chess-game-unfold.

Chapter 2

1. Steve Saccone, *Protégé: Developing Your Next Generation of Church Leaders* (Illinois: InterVarsity Press, 2012), 29.

Chapter 3

1. Daniel Martins, "Death Valley 'super bloom' dazzles in hottest place on Earth," *The Weather Network*, March 9, 2016, https://www.theweathernetwork.com/us/news/articles/us-weather-death-valley-super-bloom-dazzles-in-hottest-place-on-earth/64144/.

2. James Clear, "How Long Does It Actually Take to Form a New Habit? (Backed by Science)," *Huffington Post*, April 10, 2014, http://www.huffingtonpost.com/james-clear/forming-new-habits_b_5104807.html.

3. Alex Rosenberg, "The inspiring story of the worst market timer ever," *CNBC*, August 27, 2015, http://www.cnbc.com/2015/08/27/the-inspiring-story-of-the-worst-market-timer-ever.html.

Chapter 4

1. Joshua Harris, *Dug Down Deep: Building Your Life On Truths That Last* (Colorado: Multnomah Books, 2011), 61.

Chapter 5

1. Josh Duboff, "Ryan Gosling: 'I Think I'm A Pretty Weird-Looking Guy'," *Yahoo!*, October 4, 2011, https://www.yahoo.com/celebrity/blogs/thefamous/ryan-gosling-think-m-pretty-weird-looking-guy-115546237.html.

2. Debra Lipson, "20 Celebs You'd Never Guess Are Insecure," *The Huffington Post*, October 9, 2013, http://www.huffingtonpost.com/2013/10/09/insecure-stars_n_4072312.html.

Chapter 6

1. Michael Hyatt, "The One Thing You Must Do To Achieve Break-Through Results," *Michaelhyatt.com*, February 8, 2013, https://michaelhyatt.com/break-through-results.html.

2. Bill Johnson, *Dreaming with God: Co-Laboring with God for Cultural Transformation* (Pennsylvania: Destiny Images Publishers, Inc., 2006), 45.

Chapter 7

1. Frederick Buechner, *Wishful Thinking: A Seeker's ABC* (San Francisco: Harper San Francisco, 1993), 119.

2. Biography.com Editors, "Alfred Nobel Biography.com," *The Biography.com website*, April 27, 2017, https://www.biography.com/people/alfred-nobel-9424195.

Chapter 8

1. John C. Maxwell, *Failing Forward: Turning Mistakes Into Stepping Stones For Success* (Nashville: Thomas Nelson, 2000), 27.

Chapter 9

1. Stormy Omartian, *The Power of a Praying Wife* (Oregon: Harvest House Publishers, 1997), 169.

2. "I Have A Dream," *Wikipedia*, https://en.wikipedia.org/wiki/I_Have_a_Dream.

3. "Martin Luther King Jr. Quotes," *Goodreads*, https://www.goodreads.com/quotes/390807-use-me-god-show-me-how-to-take-who-i.

4. Keith Malcomson, "The 1859 Ulster Revival," *Pentecostal Pioneers*, http://www.pentecostalpioneers.org/1859UlsterRevival.html.

5. Evangelical Protestant Society, "Hansard Report of the debate in the Northern Ireland Assembly on the 1859 Revival - Tuesday 4 November 2008," *Ulster Bulwark*, http://archive.niassembly.gov.uk/record/reports2008/081104.htm.

Chapter 10

1. Jon Acuff, "The question a 10 year old asked me that changed how I see money," *Jon Acuff*, January 22, 2016, http://acuff.me/2016/01/the-question-a-10-year-old-asked-me-that-changed-how-i-see-money/.

Chapter 12

1. Beth Moore, *Praying God's Word: Breaking Free from Spiritual Strongholds* (Nashville: B&H Publishing Group, 2009), 20.

2. Oklahoma City Thunder, "A Message of Strength, Faith and Love." Online video clip. *YouTube*. YouTube, 18 Feb. 2016. Web. 22 June 2017.

Made in the USA
Monee, IL
07 June 2021